Go Bold

You Are Next In Line To Do
Great Things

Joel Brown

Founding Pastor Church at Hampton Roads

Go Bold is a call to action guide that moved me to awakening. No longer was it the football coach at my side telling me to get in the game, but Christ himself, reminding me of who I am. A book that actually transforms inhibitions. NO FEAR... Go Bold...

--**Gene Bunn**
Virginia Tech Football Hall of Fame 2010

"Breaking through barriers starts with your attitude; overcoming obstacles is a choice" Joel Brown. If you only have 20 minutes, read through Principle #9 – Bold People Break Barriers. It will radically change the way you start your day and meet challenges. Go Bold is an excellent book for those who want to live a life of impact. It is filled with wisdom and truths that meet you where you are and takes you on a journey that will transform your life.

--**Jeffrey W. Ganthner**, AIA, Architect
Principal and General Manager: Burns & McDonnell

As a pastor who is tempted to listen & yield to the voice of fear, I found this book to be a most valuable resource for my life and ministry. If anyone has figured out how to *Go Bold* it would be Pastor Joel. Get this book, circle up your leaders, and begin to set in motion the dreams and visions God has given you. Go Bold or go home.

--**Casey Henagan**, Lead Pastor/Founder
Keypoint Church. Bentonville, Arkansas

Go Bold is a book for anyone that needs to be reminded of who they are in Christ and needs the motivation to get moving towards the dreams and visions that fear has kept at bay deep down in their spirit. Any book that moves you to action and to do it BOLDLY is worth reading!

    --Tiffany Laitola, Master Chief. U.S. Navy

God has placed this in Joel's heart, this book will change your way of thinking and will help you to reach the destiny that God has prepared for you. He writes from his heart and the experiences that he has lived. When you decide to GO BOLD your life, your family, your city, your nation will change for the glory of God.

    --Robert Quintana, Creative Director,
      Christ for the Nations Institute

Pastor Brown gives us a simplistic guide to understanding how to break out of the bondage we are in and Go Bold. God does not call anyone into mediocrity. That is where Satan wants us to dwell. Satan knows that with boldness, God's people can achieve anything! If you read and follow the principles in this book, you too can live in peace as God intended. Go Bold is a fabulous tool to help us represent the character of God to this fallen world.

    -- **Kellie vanAvery,** Real Estate Entrepreneur
      Former ASCA Olympic Swim Coach
      US Swim Team Owner

Go Bold

You Are Next In Line To Do
Great Things

Joel Brown

Founding Pastor Church at Hampton Roads

The integrity and moral courage of the upright will guide them, But the crookedness of the treacherous will destroy them.
Proverbs 1:3 (AMP)

Dedication

To you, the reader, for whom I desire nothing more than an overflow of courage at each moment when fear is deafening.

To all who have been told they do not have what it takes, you do!

To the once fearful.

To the ones who will change the world.

To every individual, who though they haven't yet, will.

To those who have already stepped boldly and will continue on no matter the cost.

To those who have lost hope -- there is hope.

To those who will finally silence the opposition.

To every follower of Jesus, you matter.

To every person who finally realizes if they can think differently, they can live differently.

To Jesus. You make a way where there seems to be no way.

Acknowledgements

Thank You, Jesus, for life. For Your Spirit. I have nothing except what I have been given from heaven. I struggle with understanding the depth of Your love and forgiveness; however, thank You for it. Thank You for allowing me to speak into the world what You have placed on my heart. You are the light of the world and the light of my life.

To my INCREDIBLY AMAZING wife, Sarah. There are no words to express how much you inspire me. You make me better in so many ways. You have given me more grace than I deserve. There is no person on this earth or in my life who compares to you. You are one of the boldest people I know. You have stepped through things with the help of God that has caused others to crumble. You are going to speak to nations. Your story is powerful and important. There is so much in you that others have yet to see. You are beautiful, and you are mine.

To my kids. Hannah, Bethany, and Josiah, you are more than incredible. I love you three more than you will ever know! You will go farther than me, do greater things than I ever could have dreamed. Take this book to heart. Live it. Make Jesus' Name known on the earth during the time God has allotted you. You ARE world changers. Every moment counts. Be intentional and do not let anyone tell you what you can and cannot accomplish. According to your faith be it unto you.

Dad, you placed depth in me that I didn't even realize was in me until after you were gone. I miss you. I wish I had made your life easier than I did. You are the reason I love Jesus. Thank you for loving God the way you did in front of me. I will see you soon.

Mom, you are a strong woman. Always serving others. Never putting yourself first. You are the epitome of humble. I love you so much and without your example of boldness I would not have been able to accomplish this book. You are relentless, and I am forever grateful God gave you to me.

To my brother Michael. Watching you walk through your obstacles while still loving Jesus and pursuing your calling is an inspiration. I would not be who I am without you. You are phenomenal. Go bold bro. Never stop. Push, believe and reach the world. You have everything you need to go further.

Thank you to all of the staff at Church at Hampton Roads for working tirelessly on the vision God has given us as a church and for alleviating my load as I focused on getting what was on my heart out and onto these pages. There's no team I would rather do life with. You will impact the world!

To my pastors, Casey Henagan and Spencer Beach (and families). I can never tell you adequately how you and your families shaped our lives. You are models of God's grace. You loved my family in ways many will never know. And you prepared us for the future. Thank you. And thank you for continuing to pastor me and oversee me even now. I love you.

Thank you to my editor, Denise. You inspire me. You were a Godsend. Without you I would not have been able to finish this. You pushed me, encouraged me, and spoke life into this process and I look forward to writing countless books in the future with you. Thank you for not giving up on God or your gift. You were called for such a time as this!

Forward

What does being BOLD look like? Does it look different on a basketball court or other athletic field than it does in a corporate boardroom? Does it reveal itself differently on a mission field than it does in a start-up business? I say no.

We've probably all watched a sporting event or played in one where the game came down to one pivotal moment, one final shot. That is when you see boldness. You see the person who stands and wants to take the last shot while others around shrink in the moment. I see the same thing in corporate meetings in my role as a Vice President of Supply Chain Finance in the Consumer Goods industry. I see big decisions needing to be made and few people willing to stand and make a choice. I see one or two confident members make the decision for the whole group. As Joel writes in this book, they are the ones who step to the front of the line.

We reward and admire the bold. The athlete who takes the last shot, the leader who makes the tough decision, the friend or pastor who will speak truth to us. So, if we admire these people and the attributes they possess, why is it so hard for us to be bold?

In this book, the definition of boldness is provided. It is confidence, courage, and willingness to take risks. Taking a risk can lead to failure but how we view that failure is important. Do we view it as catastrophic or just a step toward success? A basketball player becomes great by practicing, and a scholar becomes great through studying. We can become great by listening to God and understanding His calling on our life. Relentlessly pursuing his calling, for His glory, with boldness and faith will give you the breakthrough you are seeking.

In the nearly 20 years that I have known Joel, one theme has been consistent; his pursuit of the purpose and calling that God placed in his life. I admire him for his boldness and know that God is using him in the authorship of this book to help others overcome the same obstacles, barriers, fear and doubt that he has overcome. I have sat with Joel at the very moments when he was weighing significant life choices in following God's calling. I have seen him choose action over inaction, insecurity and struggle over comfort and cautiousness. None of these choices and actions were made without an enormous amount of prayer and listening to God's voice.

Joel is a mentor to me and a strong leader for his family, church, and friends. It was a great pleasure to read this book and remember the times when I have seen Joel utilize the very principles he is now presenting to us. The twelve principles in this book are combined in a manner that both build upon and complement each other. Of the twelve, the one that hit home the most for me was Principle 6: Faith is the Fuel That Powers Boldness. Having faith not in who we are or what we can accomplish, but whose we are was a huge un-lock in my life.

All the times when I am overwhelmed, and the obstacles seem too big to overcome, when family and work commitments collide, when the pressure to deliver is the greatest. At these times when it seems there is no way out of my current circumstances, I quiet my mind and talk to God. I humble myself to Him and His greatness, knowing that only through Him can I overcome. Then I step with boldness knowing that He is clearing the path before me.

As I sit here today and reflect, I can see all the times when God has provided. Sometimes when I have asked, but more often when I haven't. God wants us to be successful, and when we are and bring Him the glory the blessings continue. Momentum builds. Thoughts and actions that used to be pre-meditated become unconscious habits. This book will help you realize that you can be BOLD, that you should be BOLD. Take a step of faith knowing that you are God's creation and He wants great things for you!

The need to be bold translates to every person through vocation, education, athletic endeavor, or other area. We are all called to be bold and Joel provides an excellent outline utilizing twelve principles that will help you grasp and overcome the fear that keeps us from being bold. This is not a book to be read once and put on a shelf. It contains tools to help us on a daily basis and should be used as instruction and affirmation frequently. Find the courage, face the fear and be confident in whose you are......GO BOLD!

Mark Freeburg
VP Operations Finance
Boulder Brands

Contents

Principle #10
Boldness Awakens Greater Opposition

Principle #11
The Bold Fail, But The Bold Do Not Faint!

Principle #12
Boldness is Not About Knowing Every Step, But About
Knowing The One Who Orders Your Steps

The Lagniappe Principle
Relentlessness Separates the Ones Who Make It From the
Ones Who Will Not

Introduction

What could you accomplish if you had the boldness to step through fear? Do you dream of starting your own business or writing a book or composing a song? Is your desire to be the 'first', or 'to stand up for' or 'create a new idea'? To be influential? To change culture or at least be a voice that can speak into it? Then what's holding you back?

Regrets fill those who, at the end of their life, finally come to realize missed opportunities. You see, being at the end of the time allotted for life is just like the perspective a basketball game gives you. Going into the game you do not foresee the things that will take place but towards the end; after seeing your decisions in certain key moments you begin to deconstruct what could have been if you had made different choices. You begin to think back to the first quarter, second quarter, and then your mind goes to halftime. All of the missed opportunities come flooding back into your mind. This is how life sadly goes for most. It takes most people to the end of their life to begin to regret not taking the risks necessary to make real impact.

The spirit of fear is a thief. The spirit of fear is a robber. The spirit of fear seems to be an immovable enemy that keeps you servant to its will and desires. Tremendous dreams, businesses, books, and new ideas in history have been lost simply due to the fact that the carriers of those dreams and new ideas never stepped into the realization of what they saw in their heart and mind. They end up at the end of their allotted time in life in complete regret, thinking about what could have been.

Can you start to see how the spirit of fear operates? Can you see how it paralyzes? It tells you, "Be quiet, no one wants to hear from you." It tells you, "The risk is too great just stick with what you know." It tells you, "You won't be able to finish it so why even start?" **The voice of the spirit of fear is loud for each one of us. It blares and resounds inside of us in order to keep us neutralized and marginalized.** And for the most part it accomplishes its mission -- to steal what is inside of you and me and to steal the destiny God has ultimately planned for us.

So let me ask, "Who are you? What kind of person are you?" Are you going to end up a statistic of the spirit of fear? Will you be part of the marginalized and neutralized -- the one filled with regret at the end? I believe the answer to those questions is NO! I believe God has you reading this book at just the right time! I believe the Spirit of God is going to honor your desire to live boldly, to do great things, and to be effective and influential because He's made you for those purposes! But the choice is yours. If you decide you are going to move forward, you are going to have to go bold!

Going bold is a must if you are going to make it in life and succeed. If you are going to break new ground, you must step out of your comfort zone. Because to be noticed by others, to fulfill a God-given God-sized dream, you are going to have to go bold.

What if the spirit of fear was no longer the reigning power in your life? *Mark Twain said, "Courage is not the absence of fear, but the mastery of it."* You cannot have courage without the presence of fear. You must be bold even though faced with high levels of anxiety and faced with a multitude of situations whose outcomes are unknown. Timid and fearful people are of no consequence. They do nothing in life and they do it well. Many are caught up and paralyzed by fear that they will not achieve; therefore, they try nothing. They will be forgotten by history. Talent wasted, years wasted, lives wasted, resources wasted. And the root of it all? A lack of courage.

Those who have seen breakthrough did so because they were willing to go against the flow; they believed and acted differently. This book is designed to equip and help you get out of neutral and start moving in the right direction. It's designed to empower you to break out of the labels that either you have used to define yourself, others have used to define you, or the world has used to define you. Are you paralyzed by the spirit of fear? Then know from this moment on that you do not have to be!

I wrote this book because God has led me to share with you the power behind being bold. God has asked me to do many things that would require me to step through and master my fear; to stir myself deeply and scrounge up faith to move and act when all I wanted to do at the moment is run and hide. And I am sure

> God wants you next in line to do great things and boldness is the prerequisite!

that you have had those moments too. But know that you no longer have to run and hide. Know that God is present to help you come out of the darkness. Know that you can see miracles. To walk in boldness with God means that God will show up and do the things that you and I cannot. Walking in the power of boldness is a true partnership developed between you and the Holy Spirit of God. **Matthew 19:26 "..all things are possible to those who believe."**

So...what is it you want to do? What is it you feel like God has asked you to do? Whatever it is - a dream, an opportunity, a direct call from God - know that it WILL require boldness. Paul says in *Philippians 1:20, "MY EAGER EXPECTATION AND HOPE, is that I will not be ashamed about anything, but that now as always with all boldness, Christ will be highly honored..."*[1] So, I ask you again: What is it you have been dreaming of doing? Are you avoiding the answer because of fear? Ask the question and do not be afraid of the answer because God has put that dream in your heart. If you do not pursue it in life you will, by the end of your life, have feelings of shame or regret because you did not act.

The twelve chapters within this book are written as Twelve Principles that if you allow them will release God-given boldness. The first step in going bold is understanding your need of it! You *need* to go bold. You need to live out your God-given dreams. Your friends need you to live out your God-given ideas (even if they might be skeptical). The world needs you to step up. And *God* Himself wants you to be next in line to do great things. Because He created you with a specific purpose. And boldness is a prerequisite to accomplish anything.

To help you apply the principles of boldness to your life, I have given you a place at the end of each principle to write down three practical steps you will personally decide to do to apply that principle to your life. And I have provided a prayer at the end of each principle as well. This is to help seal the work God will be doing in you. Because you can't live out what you don't have. And, at the end of the day, breakthrough depends on you coming to God with faith.

Pray this with me before you start the book.

Father, I thank You that You did not create me to be a slave to the spirit of fear, but to stand boldly in the face of opposition. To accomplish what others think to be impossible. Holy Spirit, thank you that You are calling me and are empowering me, even now, to step into the boldness You have for me. I thank you that I am next in line to do great things. In Jesus Name. Amen.

It's time to Go Bold. Are you ready? Then let's go!

Principle #1

You Can Choose at Any Point to Live & Think Bold

Freedom lies in being bold.
Robert Frost[2]

The first principle to go bold is that: you can choose to live and think bold at any point in your life. I am convinced that before we can pursue something we must define what that something is. Therefore, in order to begin the act of being bold, we need to first define the word. The word bold is an adjective (a descriptive word) meaning: "showing an ability to take risks; confident and courageous"[3]. *Boldness* by definition is not unlike the word bold but expands the concept. Boldness *is* confidence and courage and willingness to take risks.

One of the words directly associated with the word *bold* is the word *fearless*. But because we all experience fear, I do not believe we can truly live a 100% fearless life. This takes some of the pressure off. We will all experience fear's attempted grip at some point in our life. Thus, we should look at a word associated with fearless and that is the word *brave*. I believe this word gives us a glimpse into what is takes to step into true boldness. Webster's Dictionary defines *brave*

like this: "having or showing mental or moral strength to face danger, fear, or difficulty; having or showing courage".[4]

Peter, a disciple of Jesus, was bold. Even when he was absolutely wrong, he did what he did wholeheartedly. Peter cut off the ear of the high priest's servant Malchus on the night that Jesus was betrayed.[5] He rebuked Jesus, telling Him that He would not go to the cross and die[6]. Peter even cursed at the top of His lungs, denying Jesus for yet a third time after he was so sure he would never deny Jesus.[7] However, when Peter got it right he acted in all boldness as well. It was Peter who preached boldly and saw 3,000 people added to the church in one day. Imagine that! No social media, no internet, no website, and yet with just one speech he influenced and impacted 3,000 to buy into this new concept called The Church designed by a risen Savior. It was his faith, acting in the face of fear that brought the impact by the Holy Spirit.[8]

One of those who began to do life with the original Church was Stephen. Stephen was one of the first deacons of the Christian Church. Stephen had faith in Christ; he taught those around him and he performed miracles. In the end, his life was cut short; Stephen was stoned to death.[9] I am convinced that Stephen studied and picked up not only

Peter's attributes but also those of all the other disciples. He served the Lord with boldness.

Doing time around bold people who are surrendered to God does something on the inside of us. It actually begins to stir the truth in us that we too can choose at any point to live the same way! To go bold you must follow in someone else's footsteps. We instinctively follow the models that are set before us. You might have heard the statement, "Monkey see, monkey do". We live out a version of what we see in life. Stephen witnessed something in Peter. Peter's example began to stir up something within Stephen, a boldness to witness and speak out when it could cost him his life! It was transferred boldness! Do you see the transfer happening?

> We instinctively follow the models set for before us & live out a version of what we see in life. To go bold you must follow in someone else's footsteps.

Peter's boldness was the belief that he too could be a world changer like Jesus! Jesus was a revolutionary; Peter followed suit. Stephen then grasped the knowledge and truth that he as well could live without fear dictating his every move. The world had no idea of the stand Stephen was about to make on behalf of Christ and His Church, the impact his life would give to others around him, and the boldness his next life decisions would have on the Church for centuries to come.

You see, as you witness the boldness of others as Stephen did, you begin to see that fear should never hold you back. As you see the accomplishments of those who are willing to step out, and even fail, you witness eventual success. You will see impact and gain influence based on your relentless pursuit to accomplish great things. Success is achieved when you continually strive to attain, even in the face of fear.

Unfortunately, the opposite can be true as well. You might have experienced success at a specific point in your life then come face-to-face with doubt and fear. Maybe you began to fixate on the fear that resides in others, and now you are living a paralyzed life. Just because you have been bold and successful in the past doesn't mean that you are not right around the corner from fear taking hold. However, this does not mean that if you are at this moment living in the grip of fear, that you are not about to turn the corner again and break the power of doubt and fear and start doing what others deem impossible. In Matthew 9:29, Jesus is about to perform a miracle -- to open the eyes of some blind men. But before He does, He asks this question, "Do you believe I can do this?" After they responded 'Yes' He healed them and gave them what they were after. He then ended by saying, "According to your faith be it unto you."[10] Who you were yesterday does not dictate who you are today. How is your faith? If you believe in God's power, even now your eyes can be opened in order to see yourself in a different way.

Every day holds new choices. In 2011 Sarah and I, and our three children, had spent the previous few years settling into our recently purchased house in an area of Arkansas that we loved. I had a great job as worship pastor over two campuses of a thriving church; Sarah was leading children's ministry over both campuses as well; the kids all had friends and activities they participated in, and my oldest daughter was about to enter her high school years. In the midst of our comfortable life, God called us to move from Arkansas to Virginia to start a new church from scratch. To Virginia--a place over a thousand miles away from all we knew and into an area of the unknown. I didn't even know Chesapeake, Virginia, was a city that existed. I knew Virginia as a place where we knew one family and a state I had only been once to visit, two years prior. We did not have the money to start a new church. We did not have the teams to start a new church. We did not have the knowledge of the area to even know where to plant the church. We did not have any of the things people say you need to be successful. **But we had a choice.**

You see, before we knew we would succeed, before we had gathered a team to support a church plant, and before we raised the $130,000 needed to launch, we made a bold decision to do what was in our hearts -- which was to follow God, to meet Him in Virginia, be obedient, and go bold. And on September 16th of 2012, Church at Hampton Roads opened its doors with a serve team of just seventeen people (other than my family).

> Boldness says it does not matter how I lived yesterday;
> I am stepping into something new today!

Paul tells us in 2 Corinthians 5:7, "...live by faith, not by sight." Boldness says, *It does not matter how I lived yesterday; I am stepping into something new today!* Boldness says, *I don't care what it looks like, I can do it.* **Boldness says, 'Tell me what I can't do and watch me prove you wrong!'**

Sure, loading a 24-foot U-Haul and moving twenty-two hours away from everyone and everything we had known to a new place without a job or an income, and with three kids, might appear a little unsteady. I am certain that renting a house by faith (that, by the way, cost me over double what I was paying in Arkansas) and signing a six month lease on a public school to serve as our building (an additional $3,400 a month on top of the house cost) looked to some people like a dumb idea -- even foolish. But we *had* to do what was in our hearts and do it all on faith with a relentless boldness.

And God has proved faithful. As of September 17, 2017, (our five-year mark) Church at Hampton Roads has seen hundreds join the church. We have seen people grow closer to Jesus and each other through Connect Groups. We have developed outreach programs to meet the physical and spiritual needs of those in our community. Our weekly podcast is in 38 countries and over 100 regions in the US. We've leased an executive office in the heart of our city. Our staff has written its own discipleship curriculum and we have a vision to plant six more campuses in the Hampton Roads area which is also known as the Seven Cities. We received two major grants as a new church plant that allowed us to hire inner city kids to keep them off the streets! Tell me what new church has ever received grant money in its first few years! God's favor has been all over the choices we have made by faith.

No matter how many years you have suffered from the paralysis of fear you can be bold today! Nothing can stop you. The Bible says nothing is impossible to those who believe![11] Fear caused Peter to deny Jesus -- but he rebounded and became a pillar of the Christian Church. Fear may have caused you to stop dreaming -- but you too can rebound and fulfill the destiny designed by God for you. **It's time to realize that you can choose at any time to live and think bold. YOU _ARE_ the next in line to do great things!**

Action Points to Help You Choose to Be Bold:

1. _____

2. _____

3. _____

Pray this with me:

Lord Jesus, thank You for this moment. A moment where You have shown me that I am never locked into who I was in the past. That new power, new dreams, new steps are possible and that it's not too late for me. That You created me in Your likeness and You are a bold God. You left Heaven for me before I loved You in return, what a bold move. Thank You for empowering me right now Holy Spirit to take steps into my future by faith even before I see the outcome. In Jesus Name. Amen.

Principle #2

Boldness Moves You to the Front of the Line Ahead of Those Who Lack It

The doors will be opened up to those bold enough to knock.
Tony Gaskins

In the book of Acts the needs of the people were mounting quickly. The church in Jerusalem after the death, resurrection, and ascension of Jesus was growing quickly and the weight of responsibility the disciples had was mounting quickly also. Jesus had told the disciples to wait in Jerusalem for power to be His "witnesses". So they gathered in a house together, but it was not where they were going to stay.[12] The power of the Holy Spirit was going to give them boldness to go out and to go against the grain. To face fear and impact the world – and they did.

During this time there were complaints that the needs of some were being overlooked by the church. The disciples heard this and responded. In Acts 6:2-4 it reads, "It is not well that we should turn aside from preaching and teaching the word of God to sit at tables and give out money...choose from among yourselves seven good men; men who have the

Spirit of God and are wise, and we will give this work to them; so that we can spend our time in prayer and in preaching the gospel."

Now, if you remember ever playing any type of pickup game (basketball, kickball, baseball, etc.) you know that the first person chosen is always the no-brainer - that person you want on your team before anyone else. When the NFL holds their yearly draft, the first pick is the most valuable because you get the best football player there is. So, who was the first pick? Acts 6:5 tells us, "This proposal pleased the whole group. They chose Stephen, a man full of faith and of the Holy Spirit; also Philip, Procorus, Nicanor, Timon, Parmenas, and Nicolas from Antioch..." These seven who were chosen were good at what they did but faith was what Stephen was good at so Stephen stood out. He was their first draft pick.

I love the fact that it says they *chose* Stephen, a man full of faith and of the Holy Spirit. Stephen embodied boldness and that put him next in line! Fear could not keep its cold grip on Stephen. He displaced fear when it would try to grab ahold of him and that quality was recognized by all around him. He had unbridled faith. The others chosen are then listed after Stephen but no other information is given. All that is provided is their names, "...also Philip, Procorus, Nicanor, Timon, Parmenas, and Nicolas from Antioch..."

(Most likely if you are like me, the only name I remember is Stephen. And I have yet to meet someone who can list the others by memory).

The disciples found themselves in an Upper Room (Acts Chapter One) praying. They were committed to not leaving that room until they had received the power Jesus had told them about. The Upper Room was a breeding ground for what was to come next - that defining moment that would empower them to live a life that would impact and change the world. Like the disciples, you will have to decide who you are behind closed doors before you ever can influence the world. The mark of the Holy Spirit on the disciples' lives (and on the lives of those chosen), I believe, was boldness. Yes, they spoke in tongues. Yes, they prophesied. However, it's easy to do all that in a closed room with people that all think like you. It is another thing to take what you have outside to where you will be ridiculed and opposed.

> You have to know who you are behind closed doors before you ever can influence others.

The disciples ended up leaving that room. And the boldness they carried within them gave them influence to flip the world on its head. Acts 17:6 describes it this way, "These men who have turned the world upside down..." They were influencers. They were world changers. They had the truth and the truth was setting others free. The disciples carried the very power of God. They were healing people like Jesus did; they were seeing tens of thousands come to repentance and be added to the church. They were challenging the status quo that had been established by the Jewish leadership. They were succeeding in shaping history!

The Holy Spirit had been poured out onto them in the Upper Room and the ensuing boldness then took them to the streets! They went from a group that was scattered easily (like they did when Jesus was arrested - see Mark 14:50, Matthew 26:56) to unified and empowered. Through the Holy Spirit they were prophesying and speaking in languages they had never learned (and the people made fun of them and accused them of being drunks, boozers, and alcoholics--they didn't care; they kept on). They healed the sick. They built the church. They had renewed spiritual strength and it was all due to what God was doing on the inside of them. And it all came from their willingness to make the decision to step out regardless of the obstacles.

We all want to have influence and live a significant life, be a world changer, a catalyst for a revolution, and boldness is what is required in order to do that. Boldness is what propelled Peter to the front of the line into his next moment of infamy. Imagine this moment: you are in the city of Jerusalem, in the city where you have been living. You are out in public, maybe in the center of the city or town square and you have a message you want to convey. Do you go ahead and speak it out loud to everyone else standing and walking around or do you hold back? Peter did not hold back; he did not allow doubt to dictate his next steps. Acts 2:14-17 says, Then Peter stepped forward with the eleven other apostles and shouted to the crowd, "Listen carefully, all of you, fellow Jews and residents of Jerusalem! Make no mistake about this. These people are not drunk, as some of you are assuming. Nine o'clock in the morning is much too early for that. No, what you see was predicted long ago by the prophet Joel: 'In the last days,' God says, 'I will pour out my Spirit upon all people. Your sons and daughters will prophesy. Your young men will see visions, and your old men will dream dreams.'"[13]

Peter became an influencer that day. He went on to tell the people who Jesus really was, even when in that very moment, he knew he was under the very real threat of losing his own life. His refusal to bow to the social pressure drove him into a lead position in the Church; he became one who impacted the world. Peter's life gives us a picture of how boldness gives you a leg up on those who refuse to embrace it.

For boldness doesn't stay quiet and it doesn't stay put. It moves. It doesn't give in to hesitation, even in the face of the fear of the unknown; it refuses to be paralyzed.

Now, I am sure the other disciples had their moment to speak up as well when the people went on gossiping about how the disciples were drunk and out of their minds. But it is the boldness to not hesitate that wins the day. Peter stepped first, it was his refusal to hesitate that shaped the moment.

> Boldness doesn't stay quiet & it doesn't stay put. Boldness moves!

Boldness draws the line between the ones at the top and the ones that are not. It was the fact that Peter spoke up first that moved him to the head of the line of influence. It was Peter who saw 3,000 immediately converted to faith in Jesus because of that one single bold move.

Put yourself in Peter's shoes. You are behind closed doors, putting your life and soul into your next steps, going all in because you believe in what you are about to do. People catch wind of whatever it is stirring in you. Then the city, not just one person or two people, but everyone begins to laugh at you. Everywhere you go people are telling you that you are stupid, dumb, and foolish to even be thinking about much less getting ready to pursue whatever it is you are about to do. How quickly would you give up? Would you drop an idea because of the pressure from others? Have you already stopped dreaming mid-stream because of the comments or criticisms of others? Well, guess what? You still have breath in your lungs and nothing is impossible to those who believe!

Many desire to be at the front of the line when it comes to life but it is only the bold who will see the front of the line. Opportunities come for everyone, but not everyone sees them or takes advantage of them. Benjamin Disraeli, a British statesman who served twice as the Prime Minister of England in the 1880s said, "The secret to success is to be ready when your opportunity comes."[14] Some people who are given opportunities are studied; some are smart and capable. Some should be able to step out and succeed because they have the pedigree or are born into the right circumstances. But in the end, none of that is the deciding factor

> I believe that you can: step out despite opposition, break out of the mold you are being kept in; I believe you *will* rise above failure!

to success. It comes down to: can you step out despite fear and can you keep on stepping? Can you listen to your opposition daily and still move forward? Can you step onto the platform, even though you might be shaking, and speak?

Can you risk looking foolish? Can you break out of the mold that the world is trying to keep you in? I'm telling you, you can!

Someone once told me, "If you do not have the faith to believe in yourself then borrow my faith, because I believe in you." And right now I am passing that wisdom onto you! Borrow my faith in you because I believe you are the kind of person who will rise above failure and doubt! I believe that you are the kind of person who is ready to unleash your dreams and visions on the world! I believe that what is in you matters, that what is in you is vital to others, I believe that you know God is asking you to come out from the sidelines and be a world shaper. However, we all need to realize that what Thomas Edison said rings true, "...discontent is the first necessity in progress."[15]

> God doesn't need the most intelligent; He needs the willing.

The fact that you are reading this book shows you are now ready to *Go Bold* and see greater things accomplished. The secret is not always a college degree, a plaque on the wall, the right references or connections. It lies in having the faith to trust God and step out. God doesn't need the most intelligent; He needs the willing. Jesus chose fishermen who were untrained and under qualified by others standards, but they were pushed to the front of God's line because they were willing to be bold. And when you, by faith come to the front of God's line, He then releases the greatness in you - that which He placed there originally. Ultimately, He gets the glory and you get to have significance. The prophet Isaiah, in the Old Testament, was thrust into significance because of these words, "Here I am, send me."[16]

Not everyone makes it to the front of the line -- but You Can! The choice is yours. You too will have to say those words and then action must come. You too must have faith to believe; it's not enough to speak, hope, dream, and plan. You must do - even when you do not know the outcome. That is the arena of faith; that is where God moves. Unbridled faith is what allows the Holy Spirit to fill you and equip you with unbridled boldness. **Boldness moves you to the front of the line ahead of those who lack it.**

Action Points to Move You to the Front of the Line:

1. _____

2. _____

3. _____

Pray this with me:

Father God, I am ready to move to the head of the line. In front of those who refuse to move and who are content to live mediocre lives. Holy Spirit, like Stephen, I'm ready to live a bold life of faith, so that I too can be a person of influence and boldness. For Your glory, for Your honor and see the impossible become possible. In Jesus Name. Amen.

Principle #3

Boldness is Fueled by Fear
(Of The Right Things)

The remarkable thing about fearing God is that when you fear God you fear nothing else, whereas if you do not fear God you fear everything else.
Oswald Chambers

You and I, we face the same things in life and we ALL face a common enemy -- that enemy is the spirit of fear. The spirit of fear does not pick and choose; the spirit of fear is no respecter of persons. It comes after everyone with the same ferocity and with the same intent which is to reduce our lives to mere existence, repetition, and the mind-numbing mundane. John 10:10 tells us that the enemy "comes to kill, steal and destroy". The spirit of fear uses lies as one of his primary tools to accomplish his task. You have to overcome this spirit if you are going to live a life of impact led by the Spirit of God. The spirit of fear attempts to keep you hiding instead of advancing; it tries to keep you complacent when you should be confident.

Many of you are held captive to the spirit of fear. The spirit of fear is from the pit of Hell; not from God! But there's one thing that is imperative and that is to bring a distinction between the spirit of fear and healthy godly fear -- there is a difference. The spirit of fear is who you are warring against and is demonic in nature. Its aim is to cripple and torment you with the end goal of bringing you into bondage. The spirit of fear is not just a mystical force or a mere emotion or a thought; it is a spirit. It lives and breathes and has intent.

> Christ's victory gives you the power to defeat the spirit of fear & to come against demonic forces.

The lies from the spirit of fear can be extreme, even irrational with its main purpose being to prevent you from advancing for and within the Kingdom of God. Such irrational fears could include the fear of terrorism that robs your daily peace, the fear of getting a terminal illness that steals your joy, the fear of poverty that kills your hope, the fear of failure that destroys your dreams.

But there is hope. Remember, Christ gave up His life on the cross to free you from the grip of the spirit of fear. The Bible tells us that we will walk on scorpions and snakes, these are words used to reference the demonic spirits that attempt to control us. The victory of Jesus gives us the power to literally walk all over them. The Bible also says, "You will keep in perfect peace all who trust in You, all whose thoughts are fixed on You!"[17]

Yet, you need to realize that fear in itself is God-given and is not a bad thing. Most of the time when you hear the word fear you think of it as a negative. You see, fear drives your actions. It can be either positive or negative. It can be the difference between life and death.

Fear actually keeps you safe at times. Fear is a powerful motivator. There are healthy and good types of fear that instead of disempowering you actually empower you. For example, the fear of dying keeps you from driving recklessly and veering into oncoming traffic which keeps you in your lane (and allows you to live to drive another day). The fear of drowning will stop you from diving into the ocean during a hurricane. This balanced, healthy type of fear is a survival mechanism that protects you. Therefore, fearing the right things fuels life itself.

Even within the animal kingdom there is a hierarchy that is attached to this type of fear. In the jungle there is found a natural God-given fear that keeps animals alive. An elephant, though greater in size and strength than any other creature, would still not challenge the lion unless danger was sensed for one of their cubs. The tiger is a predator that fears little (except perhaps another tiger) but will back down when surrounded by a pack of animals. Respecting the natural chain of fear as God designed keeps these, and other species, from going extinct. So in turn, for us, fearing the right thing keeps us in our lane and guards our life - our visions, our dreams, our aspirations.

2 Timothy 1:7 declares, "For God has not given us a spirit of fear, but of power and of love and of a sound mind."[18] God's word is very clear. He tells you that He has not given you the spirit of fear and that you are to reject it. However, the word of God tells you that the fear of the Lord is the beginning of all wisdom. You and I cannot begin to know what the right steps are unless we fear God! God is the source of all truth. He is the source of all life. He is the author of all things. He created everything through His spoken word. What He says goes and what He says matters. When you realize He holds all power and authority and you fear violating what He has said over what anyone else has said, you begin to make choices based on the right fear. The fear of the Lord guides you into wisdom and it guides you into a bold life because there is now nothing else to fear. God gets the last word and if He says to step out of the boat and walk on water, it is the understanding that He rules the

moment where your feet hit what should be liquid yet now is a solid. If God said nothing is impossible to those who believe then what are you waiting for? Why are you fearing the lies of a fallen angel, who is bound for hell, a defeated enemy over the voice of the King over all the earth and the orchestrator of life?

It is time to fear only God. To trust Him above all else. To trust Him that in that moment of faith and boldness that you are about to step into that He will meet you there and cause you to succeed! Let's be clear here. God is telling you right now to cast-off the lies, to tell the spirit of fear to shut up in Jesus' Name. To shrug off the fear that debilitates and embrace the purposes and dreams that no one can take away from you because the Ruler of all things was the One who gave them to you.

> If God, the source of all truth & life, the Author & Creator of all things says to step out of the boat & walk on water, what are you waiting for?

Demonic forces are trying to usurp God's position. Before creation, Lucifer wanted to rise above God and be higher than Him. This didn't work out so well for Lucifer; He was thrown out of Heaven like lightning (Revelation 12:7-9). Hell stands no chance against Heaven; Satan no chance against Jesus; demonic powers have no chance over the angelic. "Then I heard a loud voice in heaven say: The salvation and the power and the kingdom of our God and the authority of His Messiah have now come, because the accuser of our brothers has been thrown out: the one who accuses them before our God day and night. They conquered him by the blood of the Lamb and by the word of their testimony, for they did not love their lives in the face of death."[19] What confidence knowing the truth brings. But still demonic forces try to coerce you to bow to them by bullying you and telling you lies. "Therefore rejoice, you heavens, and you who dwell in them! Woe to the earth and the sea, for the Devil has come down to you with great fury, because he knows he has a short time."[20] Yet know, you do not have to bow to a defeated enemy!

The fear of God is the first building block of living a life of freedom and influence. If you are going to live out a life of boldness and a life of purpose, if you are going to live out your dreams and the vision that you have for life, then you have to understand that there's something larger than the spirit of fear. It's not that there aren't other things to learn about God but the Bible says you must start with the fear of God. It is the foundation of everything. Understand this: the fear of God practically means to choose Him and His Ways.

When you do this, you will never fear ANYTHING else! The fear of the Lord is knowing you want to please Him above ALL else. The Lord promised this in Matthew 6:33, "Seek the Kingdom of God above all else, and live righteously, and He will give you everything you need."[21] He is powerful beyond comprehension.

When people came in contact with God it did not look like just a small form of reverence, respect, or just a moment of awe. It is apparent that they were terrified. When Israel came to Mount Sinai in the Old Testament, God descended on the mountain with a dark cloud and thunder and lightning; the whole mountain was smoking and shaking! Imagine that for a moment. It goes on to say that all of Israel shook in fear; they were actually trembling. John, in the book of Revelation, had come in contact with Jesus and it says he fell to the ground as if he was dead. Literally, he lost all bodily control and function.

> To live out your dreams & vision for your life boldly & with purpose, you must fear God – which means to choose Him & His ways.

When you understand the vastness and greatness of God it's out of control fear. It is not a picture of this God that you can control. He is not a genie in a bottle that you conjure whenever you need something. And it is not an issue of should I fear, should I not fear. It's just reality; the reality that whoever you are, in the moment that you truly get a revelation of God, you are going to fear Him. And here is the kicker. After your initial realization of who He is, His power and majesty, He turns around and says something so beautiful: that you are His. He says, *I made you.* He says, *I love you.* He says, *I am for you.* He says, *I will guide you.* He says, I *will empower you.* He says, *I am the one who designed you to do what is in your heart.* He says, *Do not fear.* David says in the Psalms that *the Lord is my light and my salvation who should I fear?* We need to be asking the same question? Who in the world should I fear if God Himself is working with me and has commissioned me to do what is in my heart?

I remember it was not too long ago that the Holy Spirit whispered into my ear (shortly after launching the church we are pastoring), "Joel, there is no giant, no Jordan River, and no Judas that can keep you from what I have called you to do." You need to realize this as well. Goliath could not stop David. The Jordan River could not keep the Israelites out of the Promised Land, and Judas could not stop the power and destiny of Jesus! So the truth you must default to and realize is this: if God is for you who can stand against you? Absolutely no one. Who or what should you fear? Absolutely no one and no thing. **Do not go another minute without** recognizing the greatness of God and His commitment and desire to empower you.

Action Points to Fuel Fear of the Right Things:

1. _____
2. _____
3. _____

Pray this with me:

Forgive me Lord Jesus for not slowing down enough to really understand Your greatness or Your power. For living casually instead of being humbled by the thought You. I choose to tremble at the thought of You and Your word, not at the opinions of others. You are the source of all truth and power, thank you that no Goliath, no Jordan River, and no Judas can keep me from my destiny in You. No obstacle is too big.

Principle #4

Boldness is An Attribute of Those Who Spend Time in God's Presence

More is accomplished by spending time in
God's presence than anything else.
Heidi Baker

There is something about the presence God that changes us, that transforms us. Throughout the Bible, God is always trying to get close to us. He has, and always will, desire proximity. In Genesis 3:8 we see Adam and Eve recognize the sound of the Lord God walking in the Garden right after they had eaten the forbidden fruit. They were used to hearing the sound of God walking in the Garden. Adam and Eve knew the sound! It was familiar to them; they did not have to second guess what that sound was. The reason, I believe, is because the Lord God would regularly come and walk in the Garden, so the sound of His presence was recognizable. Adam and Eve were not looking at each other with confused looks on their faces asking, 'Do you hear that sound? What is that?'

Then after the relationship between God and humanity was broken with the eating of the fruit, God raised up a leader in Moses and had him build a tabernacle. The tabernacle was a temporary housing for God's presence; a place for Him to be close to us, His creation. You see, it's in the Old Testament book of Exodus that the tabernacle was a conduit for God to live among His people. Again, God was looking for a way to be close, not only because He wanted to be close but because He knew His people needed Him to be close. **God is the source of life and power and without Him we are dead; He is aware of this even if we are not.**

As you move into the New Testament, John 1:14 says that the Word was made flesh and made His dwelling with us. No longer would God exist in the Holy of Holies (the tabernacle) where only the priest could go in once a year, but that God would now interact with His creation more closely. Ultimately Jesus would live in all of us that choose Him, by His Spirit, and never leave us. God's presence would move from a tabernacle to being readily available because His Spirit would live in our very own body. This changes everything!

Of course, it is easy to be bold when you are God because then there is nothing above you, nothing greater than you, nothing stronger than you. The words You (God) speak changes reality and creates universes. Fear can't exist in the heart of God because of who He is. Genesis states that you are made in His image and in His likeness; you were created to be God's representative on Earth! That means you are created to exercise the same demeanor and authority in your life. After all He did tell man to subdue the earth. Simply put, make sure everything you experience in life and anything you come across does not subdue you.

However, something happened. Man became captive to pride, fear, anxiety, discouragement, depression, and worry. And with that lost the power to represent the power and authority of God on earth because humanity after the Garden was separated from God. This is the power of the cross! The cross is the hinging point. Jesus, God in the flesh, through His very own body, made a new and living way for us to be restored and

> You were designed to represent the character of God here on earth. If God isn't threatened by fear and Heaven isn't worried, then you shouldn't be either!

reconciled to God! That restoration of proximity would restore your understanding of your identity, your original design and your original purpose - to rule and take authority over the earth and to represent the nature and character of God on this planet. If God is not threatened by fear and if Heaven itself is not worried, then once you get back into proximity with Him you begin to act as He acts, move as He moves, and fear loses its dominating grip on you. His DNA begins to lodge itself in you again and you become the one telling fear where to go, telling doubt it has no power over you. You have been renewed into the likeness and image of your Creator and have been reminded He left you the authority to rule. In other words, when you begin to spend time with God, He begins to restore your DNA. He begins to call out of you what was dormant - your true identity in Him. Romans 12 says that you are to not be conformed to this world but be transformed by the renewing of your mind. To renew means to resume (an activity) after an interruption.

That's what happened! Your connection to an all-powerful Creator was interrupted by man thinking he had a better plan. This is what Lucifer fell to also, pride and ultimately rebellion. In what I believe to be one of the most satanic songs ever written, "My Way"[22] sung by Frank Sinatra, there is a line that says, "I planned each charted course, each careful step along the byway. And more, much more than this, I did it my way." Each of us was influenced and lied to by Satan himself and took the bait of thinking we could do it our own way, stripping us of our proximity to God. We took on the nature of and character of the kingdom of Satan. Much like we were created to represent God's

Kingdom, we became representatives of the Kingdom of darkness.

This Kingdom consists of confusion, fear, bitterness, worry, discouragement, depression, guilt, perversion, lust, greed, divisions, and shame. When you are living out these attributes in your life you need to realize these are the characteristics of a different Kingdom living in you rather than the Kingdom of God. Spiritual demonic forces have proximity and access to you rather than the Spirit of God. Ephesians 6 states clearly that your battle is not against flesh and blood, but against rulers, authorities, powers of darkness and spiritual forces in the heavens. It's time to give your heart, your time, your devotion back to God. And then His Kingdom is allowed access again because you are spending time with Him in worship, prayer, and fasting.

Jesus said the Kingdom of Heaven is like yeast; it will permeate everything! Yeast is alive. It changes the consistency of that which it is touching. The same can be said for God Himself. As His presence is allowed in, He replaces the demonic influences you face. Where you were once bound to fear and failure, He changes you and you can, just like Gideon - an original coward - lead 300 men against over 100,000 with just clay jars and torches[23]. And win the battle! For you were never created to be dominated by fear. You were created to be like God. And those who make the reconnection are empowered because it is impossible to connect to the Giver of Life and not be empowered. You end up receiving again the attributes of God. You do not become God, but you become like Him - bold, empowered, loving, forgiving, persistent, relentless, and committed to what is in your heart!

Look at what the Bible says about Peter and John in Acts 4:13, "When they saw the courage of Peter and John and realized that they were unschooled, ordinary men, they were astonished and they took note that these men had been with Jesus." The rulers and elders of the people in Jerusalem had just dealt with Jesus. They had dealt with His boldness to go into the temple and flip the tables of the moneychangers over, to break social norms (even though He was not supposed to) and talk to the Samaritan woman, to debate the teachers of the law and stun them with His understanding, and how He continued to redefine the world around Him. And all this coming from a carpenter from Nazareth. He was a world changer though He was from a no name city with a common upbringing. But *they* did not define who Jesus was! The same with the disciples; the leaders saw they were "ordinary men" but that they had been with Jesus. They were displaying attributes they had only seen in Jesus, God in flesh! That same boldness He displayed. They witnessed that the disciples were being renewed into who God originally designed them to be - like Him.

It is only in the presence of God you are made new and whole. When people came in contact with Jesus, like the woman with the issue of blood who had suffered for over a decade who had exhausted every possible way of getting better, they were healed, strengthened and emboldened. Just because of the encounter with Jesus. The same happens today. The Creator of all things wants to be close to you. The One who is not fearful of anything wants you to go bold! The Author of Life wants to author a new story with you!

If you are still breathing and reading this book it is not by chance. It is because you are next in line to do great things! Push into the presence of God. Spend time in God's word, spend time praying daily, and spend time being still and listening for His voice! Make time for Him before anything else; spend time worshipping Him, understanding who He is through scripture, and then do the greatest thing you could ever do - stay in close relationship with His Spirit! Talk to the Holy Spirit, learn about the Holy

> The mark of the Holy Spirit on the followers of Jesus is unfettered boldness!

Spirit; ask for more of His Holy Spirit. Because the mark of the Holy Spirit on the followers of Jesus was unfettered boldness! **However, one thing to remember is timing!** Just because you think you are ready to jump out and take on the world, God's timing is key! God's word is power, and you should always be acting and moving in response to God's word. It is then you will have breakthrough power and faith.

Scripture tells us that faith comes by hearing and hearing by the word (*rhema*: spoken word) of God. To be bold you need faith. To have faith you must hear God. Do not launch out without faith or without a word from the Holy Spirit. This is ill advised. Take your concerns and problems to Him, take your fears to Him, He will speak to you about them, remind you who you are, and show you how to breakthrough and go bold. Seek after Him much like the disciples (in private); then you will be ready to revolutionize in public. Don't ever forget though, that He is the source. Stay desperate for Him. Stay in love with Him. He wants to partner with you in all you do. Joyce Meyer says it like this, "Spending time with God is the key to our strength and success in all areas of life. Be sure that you never try to work God into your schedule, but always work your schedule around Him."

Sometimes you will hit a roadblock, something you do not understand, and the answer is only going to be revealed when you are in God's presence. Charles Spurgeon said, "If you wish to know God, you must know His Word. If you wish to perceive His power, you must see how He works by His Word. If you wish to know His purpose before it comes to pass, you can only discover it by His Word." It is only from the presence of God that you can move forward in boldness. It is only after spending time with the Maker who fears nothing and that is over everything that you too can be emboldened.

Action Points to Help Me Spend More Time with God:

1. _____

2. _____

3. _____

Pray this with me:

Lord Jesus, I want You to rub off on me. I want the atmosphere of Heaven to be the atmosphere of my heart and life. God, fear has no hold on You or Your Kingdom. As I seek You first every day and spend time with You, I thank You that Your presence will overcome the things that once overcame me, my fear and discouragement. Thank you that even now boldness is rising and what is in me will not be contained any longer.

Principle #5

Boldness is Not a Characteristic of the Alone and Isolated Because... Boldness Rubs Off!

Courage is contagious. When a brave man takes a stand,
the spines of others are often stiffened.
Billy Graham

You have probably heard the expression 'A man is known by the company he keeps'[24]. It is true. People can shape more than just the outcome of situations; they shape you. **Those around you have great impact on your worldview, future, and ultimately your potential.** I heard it said, *"The well you drink from is the well you think from. And the well you think from determines what you will become."*[25] **Be mindful of the people you listen to (the ones that are around you) because whether you know it or not, they are influencing you.** They are shaping you more than you know. Relationships always come with the exchange of ideas, thoughts, and views. And no matter how much you may want to guard against certain ways of seeing yourself, over time you have a tendency to subconsciously take on other people's perspective without even knowing it.

You must understand that life ends up being a battle that takes place in the mind. The process goes like this: you must be careful how you think because your thoughts become your words. You must be careful of your words because your words become your actions. You must watch your actions because your actions become your habits. You must watch your habits because your habits then become your character. Finally, you must watch your character because your character determines your destiny!

In the Old Testament Scriptures, God was giving the nation of Israel instructions of all kinds. When you read Deuteronomy Chapter 20, God is giving instructions to Israel concerning how to go into battle. Verse one starts out with God telling Israel that when they go out to war and they see their enemies with their horses and chariots, and an army larger than their own, not to be afraid of them. The priest would then come out and address Israel. The priest would say things like *do not be cowardly, do not be afraid or terrified because the Lord your God is the one who is going out to fight for you, and He will give you the victory.* Then you get to read what the officers of the army would say. Deuteronomy 20:8 says, "Then the officers will also say, 'Is anyone here afraid or worried? If you are, you may go home before you frighten anyone else.'"[26] This story says a lot about people. It shows the power of influence. Ever noticed when people are happy around you, you start leaning towards feeling happy? Or when people around you are stressed out it can cause stress to rise up in you? This is what God was addressing with Israel! The officers of the army were telling those who could not find it in themselves *to be bold to go home*! They did not want those ruled by fear to be anywhere around those who actually had courage. Why? Because fear rubs off. They knew this. God knew this; which is why this concept and these instructions are in scripture.

If you want boldness you need to hang around the bold; let that boldness rub off on you! If you want courage, you need to find and spend time with courageous people! If you want to break the back of the spirit of fear, find those who have successfully defeated this spirit in their own lives! You will find yourself saying things like *if they can do it I can do it*. You will start to see the way to live out a bold life. Why? Because you start to think like them.

Jesus knew the authority He had as God in the flesh - over Satan and over the demons that He confronted. He was not scared. He knew He could tell them to go and they would. The disciples, untrained and unqualified by most standards, originally did not understand that one day they too would square off against the powers of Hell and take authority over them. They were fishermen and tax collectors, but after spending three years around Jesus, He had influenced them. He had changed the way they were thinking which changed their words, which changed their actions, which changed their habits, which changed their character, which ultimately changed their destiny. They became powerful and influential, all because of the power of proximity. The proximity and time they spent with Jesus changed them. In the same way the people and relationships you have change you - for better or for worse. And like the disciples, I am convinced that you must learn to spend time around Jesus as well. This relationship is the most important when it comes to living boldly. As Jesus, His Word and His Spirit, influences you on a daily and even hourly basis, you are changed.

> If you want:
> - Boldness – hang around the bold
> - Courage – spend time with the brave
> - To break the spirit of fear – find those who have overcome.
>
> Boldness rubs off!

What if you actually heard and felt the Spirit of the Creator of all things whisper to you, "Don't fear." Let me just tell you...It would mold you. It would shape you. It would change you! Just like it did the disciples. They were so bold they too cast out demons just like the One they hung around, Jesus. The disciples stood against whole populations of cities, all of them (except for John) ultimately were martyred in horrific and gruesome ways, which was the ultimate act of boldness. Paul was so bold he was stoned nearly to death by the men of Lystra (in Acts Chapter 14) but then got up and went straight back into the same city! I believe some of Paul's boldness came from watching Stephen, the first Christian Martyr who died by stoning early in the book of Acts. Watching Stephen die for his love for Jesus, I believe, was one of the experiences that first rubbed off on Paul. And his encounter with the risen Jesus then prepared him to do great things. When you really want to stand up

If you make the voice of God one you listen for daily, it will:
- Mold you
- Shape you
- Change you!

for something and then you see someone else stand up and lead the way, you are emboldened. I love how this is further exampled in Philippians 1:14. Paul says, *"And because of my imprisonment, most of the believers here have gained confidence and boldly speak God's message without fear."*[27] Do you see it again here? Boldness rubbing off? Paul is clear about saying it was him being in chains and modeling boldness to those who were in relationship with him and hung around him, that gave them the courage to live more boldly! What if some of those people had cut Paul off relationally before they had the opportunity to see him model such courage? They would have missed out on the impact of that moment.

I want you to think for a moment about the power of a buddy. I believe buddies lead to new beginnings. What do I mean by that? If you think back in your life to that moment where maybe you did something you never thought you would do, most likely you had a buddy present. I remember smoking my first cigarette in 6th grade and guess what, a buddy offered it to me. I remember seeing my first pornographic magazine at eleven and guess what, a buddy offered it to me. My life became incredibly hard especially after that moment - I became addicted to pornography. The power of a moment. The momentary influence of someone who was in proximity. Their trajectory in life became mine for years; that trajectory of living, meaning living life addicted, followed me into my marriage and into me being a father. Oh, the power of relationships! I wish I could go back in time and choose different people to do life with. If I had understood that things rub off I would have chosen more wisely. I didn't want to be addicted in life; I didn't get up that morning and say, 'Hey, let's make the next decade a living hell and choose addiction.' No, something rubbed off on me in a moment, in a split second! And that is how life works. That is how influence works. It only takes a split second, the right or wrong thing said...and your whole life changes.

You might have a friend who says, *You'll never be able to do that, don't try.* And over your entire lifetime those words become a prison cell. Your whole life's trajectory determined by one close friend's influence. Or it could be the opposite. One person looks you in the eye and says, *Anything is possible; go for it; I believe in you.* And that one interaction changes how you see and live out the rest of your life.

I hope you are catching the importance of choosing who gets to be close to you. It matters. 1 Corinthians 15:33 reminds you, "Do not be deceived: 'Bad company corrupts good morals.'[28] The company you keep can shape more than just the outcome of a situation. The individuals you associate with can shape who you are and who you become. So, ask yourself, 'Who are my buddies? Who has access to my mind? Who can speak into

> The company you keep can shape more than just the outcome of a situation. They can shape you!

my ears? Who is giving me advice and leading me?' The Bible says the one who walks with the wise will become wise, but a companion of fools will suffer harm.[29] Stuff is going to rub off on you. The question is, what?

So, you struggle with fear? Who around you is bold? Get around them. Don't know anyone like that? Then that is part of the problem. So, find them. Who around you is feeding your fears? Get rid of their influence. If they are in your own family, then love them, forgive them, but stop taking what they say seriously; it's not from God. Cut them off if you have to. God says that you are an overcomer! He says He has equipped you! He says He is with you and will guide you! He says nothing is impossible to those who believe! This is not complicated; choose the right voices, people, and influencers and you will be propelled into boldness!

Jesus said *I only do the things I see My Father doing.* The Father was the main source of influence for Jesus. And the Holy Spirit was the One guiding Jesus. The Holy Spirit in the Bible is represented at times as oil. I do not know if you have ever had your hands covered in oil, but it rubs off on everything! Stays on you, transfers to everything you touch. Jesus leaned on the Holy Spirit to lead Him and guide Him as His number one relationship. You must do this too. Ask the Holy Spirit to lead you as He led Jesus. Ask Him to reveal things to you, to show you the things that need to shift. Let the oil of the Holy Spirit rub off on you. Tell the spirit of fear it has no place anymore in Jesus Name! You have authority over fear. You may not think you do, but you do. Luke 10:19 says, "I (Jesus) have given you authority to trample on snakes and scorpions and to overcome all the power of the [your] enemy."[30] You do not have to be a scholar to understand what the word *all* means. Jesus said you have the authority over all of your enemies.

Are you scared? You don't have to be. Are you worried? You don't have to be. Are you anxious? You don't have to be. Are you paralyzed by doubt? You don't have to be! No enemy can stand between you and your calling, between you and your purpose, between you and your future! The only thing powerful enough to do that is you! If you think you can't, you can't.

> No enemy can stand between you & the purpose, the calling, & the future God has for you – except YOU!

Scripture says that according to your faith be it unto you. Get faith! How? Paul said, "Faith comes by hearing and hearing by the word of God."[31] The word in the Greek for *word* used here is *rhema*, meaning the spoken or uttered word. Not the black and white words on a page, but an uttered word. So why do you not have faith to be bold? You have not sought God earnestly enough to hear Him utter something to you.

You see, going back to the principle of this chapter, boldness is not a characteristic of the alone and isolated because...Boldness Rubs Off! You can't manufacture in yourself the boldness you need. You must find a place where boldness can be transferred to you. And the first place to look, instead of to people on earth, is to the Maker of Earth. God still speaks. Make time to get alone and pray, fast, and worship Him. Then be quiet and listen for Him. Heaven will speak and the power of Heaven will rub off on you and then transfer to the world around you. And finally, guard your earthly relationships. Who is closest to you, they will shape you! **If you want to be bold get around the bold.**

Action Points to Encourage Me to Associate with Others Who Are Bold are:

1. _____

2. _____

3. _____

Pray this with me:

Lord Jesus, I am asking You to guard me from isolation. From retreating from the right relationships. Put me around people who are bold! Help me to know who to spend time with. Reveal to me those who You are asking me to limit my time around because their influence is inhibiting me not helping me. Spirit of Power, Spirit of God, fill me right now with You. In Jesus Name.

Principle #6

Faith is the Fuel That Powers Boldness

*Faith is taking the first step
even when you don't see the whole staircase.*
Martin Luther King, Jr.

I grew up loving fast motorcycles. I remember telling my parents early on in my life that I wanted to get one. They kindly told me that when I turned eighteen and could afford to get one on my own that they would allow it. I could see it was going to make them incredibly nervous. However, the day came that I turned eighteen and I went out and bought my first motorcycle - a 1993 GSXR 600. (And yes, I am obviously still around.) Now it's common knowledge that just sitting on a motorcycle and wishing it would go does not make this happen. If a vehicle is going to move, it has to have fuel to power it. In the same regard, if you are going to move, if you are going to be bold in life, if you are going to look life straight in eyes and forge ahead, you too will have to have fuel. That fuel will empower you to move.

It was a bright, sunshiny day in Northwest Arkansas and I was riding my new GSXR on the highway headed home from meeting with some friends when I felt the engine momentarily sputter. It caught my attention but then it was gone and everything seemed to be fine so I kept riding. After a few more seconds it sputtered again, then again. At this point I had a sneaking suspicion I was about to be out of gas. You see, back in 1993 most bikes, including mine, did not have fuel gauges; you just had to *know* how much gas was in your tank by tracking your mileage. So, what did I do? I twisted the throttle wide open to gain as much speed as I could, so I could go as far as I could. (And yes, laws were broken. Remember I'm eighteen at this point.) The engine went silent. All I heard and felt was the sound and the resistance of the howling wind as I was losing speed. I took my exit, but it was obvious - I was going to be stranded. I had nothing left in the tank and because of that I was moments away of being on the side of the road. Then it happened, my bike came to a slow stop halfway off my exit. And there I sat, cars speeding by one after another, and me with no current way of getting to where I was heading. This is how life works. It is when you run out of fuel that you are in trouble.

If you have been alive for any length of time you have had that moment where you ran out of gas. I am speaking figuratively. I am speaking about your drive, passion, and courage to go on. You experienced that sinking feeling as you began to slow down and all you could do is look for a place to come to a complete stop to try to catch your breath and figure out what to do next. You're stranded on the side of the road of life as everyone is passing by you. They are heading to where they are going while you are at a standstill, motionless in life, due to your present situation. Maybe you are watching others live out their callings, live out their purposes, live out their hopes and dreams -- and there you are a mere bystander. You have ran out of fuel. This is a hopeless feeling, isn't it? You are not even sure how to begin to get moving again. You don't even know where to start.

You are not alone. Many are in that place right now; many need to hear their engines fire and rev up again, to experience new dreams and visions, or to see the resurrection of the ones they have been holding on to. I think it is easy to become overwhelmed when you look at all of life as one big unmanageable task. **Life can paralyze you. Your motivation and hope dwindles and so does the boldness needed to step out when faith runs out.** So ask yourself right now: 'How much fuel do I have?' Are you low or do you not have any at all? How is your forward progress? Are you stranded on the side of the road with an engine that stopped running? Here is another question. What octane are you running? You might have fuel but it might be a low grade. Your engine is running, you are moving but there are some knocks in the engine. You're not experiencing the power that comes with higher octane. Maybe it's time to upgrade the octane level of your fuel. After all, the Bible tells us that the Kingdom of God is not just about words but about power! And that power is at your fingertips. Jesus said, "Repent (think differently), for the Kingdom of Heaven is at hand." Meaning

> Your engine is about to fire up with the dreams and visions God has given you; if you believe.

that the Kingdom of Heaven is within your grasp even if you are feeling empty, dead, and lifeless!

Whoever you are, I believe your engine is about to fire up again! That new visions and dreams are about to come to you! That the dreams you have been holding on to that you know are God given are about to be resurrected. I know that you are next in line to do great things as you choose to believe. Now, you might say things in response to that like: *But you don't understand what just happened; you don't know what I did. You don't get how depressed I feel.* None of that matters now. Remember Principle One? **You can choose at any point to live & think bold!** Your past does not determine your future; who you were does not dictate who you will be; where you have been does not have to be where

73

you stay! What you need is faith. **Because faith is the fuel that powers boldness.**

Jesus says that if you have the faith the size of a mustard seed you can look at mountains and tell them to move. The obstacles you see are no match for the power of Heaven. When you actually believe God created you to have the authority to move mountains, you will begin to do so. God made man to subdue the earth, to put it under his authority; we saw this earlier in Genesis. Again, God did not intend for the things of this world to subdue us, to bring us under its authority but it was to be the other way around.

Your past does not determine your future. Let faith fuel you today!

The question is, can you get back to understanding who God made you to be? You are called to be His, and by being His, He authorizes you to live by faith and speak to the things opposing your calling and your purpose. God authorizes you to remind the world that it, nor any force of Hell, has any power to control you or to keep you down. God authorizes you to remind the world and Hell itself that intimidation won't work anymore, that there is an awakening going on inside of you and you will no longer stand and accept the lies about why you can't do the things God made you to do. **Tell the obstacles in front of you:** *I will start my business! I will accept that position even though it intimidates me! I will start that ministry! I will step out!*

So where do you get the faith to do this? Although I've hinted at this before in this book, let me now truly unpack this concept. Romans 10:17 says, "So then faith comes by hearing, and hearing by the word of God."[32] Did you catch it? Faith is a result of hearing. If I tell you there is a screaming teenager in the room next to you, but you don't hear the screaming teenager you will doubt that there truly is one. However, if I tell you there is a screaming teenager in the room next to you and you hear the sounds of that screaming teenager, you now have assurance that what I said is true. Faith is a result of hearing. But you might say, *I read the Bible; I listen to God's Word every Sunday. I listen to my audio Bible daily and yet still I am stranded in doubt and fear.* That is because that's not hearing. Although hearing scripture is important, there is a difference between hearing words third party and you having a personal interaction with the Writer of those words. Actually, hearing that Writer (God) speak verbally in the same room as you changes everything.

Let me remind you of something. Language for you and I is symbolic. The words you and I speak, the sounds that are coming out of our mouths, only symbolize a reality. If I say the word *car*, you know I am expressing a sound that symbolizes a real object that is in my garage. However, you must think differently about God's words. When God speaks it *is*. When God speaks it is not symbolic; it *is* reality! So, if God says the word *car*, a *car* is the result. His voice brings it into being.

Now, going back to this verse stating faith comes by hearing, and hearing by the word of God. You must understand something: there are two words in the Greek for the word *word*. The first is *logos*; this is the written Word of God - Scripture. The second word is the word *rhema*; this is the spoken Word of God. Guess which form is used in Romans 10:17? You guessed it! *Rhema*! You and I do not receive faith by reading the Bible. Wait! Don't shut down! Think about it. How many people have read the Bible and remained atheist, become atheist, or entertained atheism? Atheism is merely disbelieving that there is a Creator God and that all there is is what's natural - what we can see and experience physically. Just seeing the written word or even memorizing the written word is not a sure-fire way to faith. What do you need on top of knowing, reading, and memorizing scripture to experience life once again? The actual voice of God speaking to you! That is why if someone tells you "be at peace" during an incredibly difficult time, you don't always find that peace. That is because those words, unless God is actively speaking through that person to you, are merely symbolic - even if they are quoting the l*ogos*, the written Word, Scripture!

But, if you get alone and quiet with God, you seek His voice, and give Him time to literally give you a *rhema* word (a directly spoken word from His Spirit to yours) faith is the result! Because you *heard* His word. And hearing a *rhema* word is where faith is birthed, sustained, and released. So when God communicates literally, through His Spirit, the words "be at peace", the creative power of the voice of God now impacts you and the paralyzing grip of fear is broken!

The question is then how does God speak? He does speak - through time in His word, the Bible. He does speak - through teachers and pastors. He does speak - when you are listening to your audio Bible. What matters is that you know the difference between hearing audio waves from headphones and hearing audio waves from Heaven. **It is possible to have information without revelation.**

When you are reading the Bible and a verse leaps off of the page and roots itself in your heart and you can tangibly feel a shift internally, you have just experienced the *logos* moving to *rhema*. The written word has now come alive and

God has spoken that as a revelation into your soul. And the result is love, joy, peace, patience, and all of the other fruits of the Spirit that are in Galatians chapter five. You do not have to be the source of faith. Faith is a natural outflow of hearing. You can't conjure up faith. Faith is a result of hearing God speak. And yes, God still speaks.

I have never had the opportunity to hear the audible voice of God, but I know when His Spirit is speaking to my spirit. My insides explode with faith, fear diminishes, boldness rises up, love for people is aroused, and I begin to see how to step through life's craziness.

Proverbs 3:5-6 says to trust in the Lord with all your heart and in all your ways acknowledge Him and He will direct your steps. Someone who is going to lead you is going to communicate with you. The key is having an open ear daily for the *rhema* of Heaven, the spoken words of Heaven that have your name written all over them.

> Faith comes from hearing God speak – through His Word, His Spirit, teachers, and pastors.
> God speaks – get alone with Him & let Him speak Through His Spirit to yours.

This is your moment! You can make time to get alone with God; you can learn to hear His voice and even if you already do you can learn it to a new level. And as you hear God, your God given purpose will stand to its feet and present itself. And as you hear, your tank will be filled again; your octane level will go up. Your faith will be potent. And it is by faith that you will speak to your circumstances and see them changed. It is by faith you will speak to the forces of Hell itself and see them run.

Because Joshua heard God tell Him "Be strong and very courageous" he was able to say the following, "Joshua told the people, 'Consecrate yourselves, because the Lord will do wonders (mighty things) among you tomorrow.'"[33] You see, you can't do mighty things, but God can through our consecration. To be consecrated simply means to be God's. To belong to Him. To be of the mind that no other has you but Him. Basically, you are off the market much like a woman who gets engaged that will never turn her back on her fiancé. And when you draw close to God because you want Him alone, the Word says He draws close to you. And trust me, when God draws close to you He speaks. And when He speaks things are created, things shift, life is birthed.

So, Joshua tells them the secret to the next day's miracles (plural) is going to be simply: draw close to God, humbly, so that He can bring the victory on their behalf. When you realize life can now be simplified to resting in who

God is, loving Him only, responding to His leading, then all the pressure is off. That means miracles are in store and your story and purpose are secure, because He is the one carrying the weight. What boldness this now delivers to your heart!

Summed up: The power is in close relationship, not in pursuing your dreams alone. The truth is that God does not do amazing things for others so that you can just say look at what He did for them and say, *'They must be special*. NO! God does not play favorites! He does amazing things for others so that He can communicate to you these words: *I CAN DO THE SAME FOR YOU!! You are next in line to do great things if you can hear My voice. I made YOU to be a champion. I made YOU to overcome. I made YOU to be a world changer!* God is saying, "Come join the story! I have a role and a part for YOU to play."

> Stop judging your capabilities by your circumstances. Your future is based on your now!

You are most likely sitting and reading this book with an obstacle in your way, something that is keeping you from doing or being what you know you are supposed to be. It might be finances, trouble in your marriage, physical health, mental health, hopelessness - you name it. But God is telling you to believe He is a living and active God who desires to speak to you. To move you from stranded to soaring. Stop judging what you can or cannot do because of your current circumstances! Stop judging what you're capable of by what you have only accomplished to this point! Stop judging what you will have in your future based upon what you have now! My wife grew up in a two-bedroom trailer with a total of seven family members. She suffered ten years of sexual abuse and now is pastoring a healthy church alongside of me and God has blessed us with a healthy marriage and three beautiful kids who love Jesus. And guess what she now has? A home of her own!

Faith is the fuel that powers boldness. You must remember: the one who comes to God must believe that He is, and that He IS the REWARDER of those who diligently seek Him. Make time for God starting today. Seek HIM FIRST. Don't be satisfied with a day without hearing something from Him. Do this and you WILL begin to hear His Spirit. Be desperate. After all, He is the Vine and we are the branches. You have no life without God. John 3:27 says that no one has received a single thing but that what he/she has received from Heaven. You need to hear Him. Make room; He will start speaking. And your faith will soar and you will hear and feel your internal engine fire up again.

Action Points to Strengthen My Faith to Power My Boldness:

1. _____

2. _____

3. _____

Pray this with me:

Father, I thank You that You speak. I thank You that You have given me the ability to hear You and that Your word says You do not play favorites. Thank You that I have the same access to You as Moses, as Gideon, and as each of the disciples and that You desire to speak to me as you did to each of them. Speak, I am listening. I rebuke every distraction in Jesus Name that would hinder me from hearing the voice of my Creator. Holy Spirit do in me what I cannot do in myself, increase my capacity to hear. And thank You for the faith that is even now stirring in me as a result of Your presence. Amen.

Principle #7

Trust Sustains Boldness

*Never be afraid to trust an unknown future
to a known God.*
Corrie Ten Boom

The spirit of fear can be overpowering and erase any sense of boldness that may be stirring within you. We have to revisit again the fact that the type of fear that paralyzes you and stunts your faith is a demonic spirit. It is a person without a physical body who is speaking to you about who you are and what your future holds but everything that the spirit of fear says is contrary to what God has said.

Your biggest battle is spiritual. God has clearly said that you do not battle against flesh and blood; you fight against wicked spirits that only want to lure you away from Him and your original purpose, design, and ultimately your God given dreams. Refusing to bow to the spirit of fear allows you to enter what God has for you and Hell itself loses ground on this earth and the Kingdom of God expands and people are set free!

It all hinges on this...you have to learn to trust God. It is trusting God that unlocks intimacy with God. It is intimacy with God that allows you to relate and be close to Him. It is that closeness and proximity that allows you to receive His Spirit instead of the spirit of fear. And scripture tells what happens when the Spirit of God shows up. The Prophet Joel disclosed that there were two distinct results from the Holy Spirit being poured out on people: dreams & visions. You need to not miss those two key ingredients that come from intimacy with God (dreams and visions). And boldness arises in the person who is filled with an large, uncontainable vision.

Think about this, if today you could settle your absolute trajectory, your final purpose and direction, how much quicker would you step towards it? Jesus told us that the Holy Spirit would show us things to come! The problem is that at times our ears could be more attune to the spirit of fear who wants to join in and tell us what he thinks is to come. Here is the crux of the matter, who do you trust? The answer to that question determines which spirit (the spirit of fear or the Spirit of God) is allowed to lead you and feed you with what they have to offer.

Have you ever noticed when you get around someone that what is in them spills onto you? If you happen to be around a happy person who is thankful for everything, you begin to get a taste of what they are full of and it affects you. You become happier and more thankful. However, if you get around someone who is cynical and bitter and hates life, over time you begin to experience life the way that they do because they can only give to you what they are full of inside! Now, the same is true with spirits. Spirits do have proximity to you whether you like that idea or not. Whether you believe that or not, they do. God has said this in His Word. And spirits, much like people, are full of things that overflow onto you when they come close to you. And, much like people, they can only share with you what they are full of - what is in them is all they have to offer. Just like that person you hang around can only offer you what is inside of them (whether it's joy or depression), you are going to receive who they are on the inside. This is why if you are constantly fearful to step and be bold in what God has called you to do - you have been affected by a life lived intimately with the spirit of fear. You

> The spirit you trust —
> the spirit of fear or the
> Spirit of God —
> determines the dreams,
> visions, & direction
> of your life.

have allowed this spirit, person without a physical body, to be in your personal space. The result is you have received the substance of the spirit you have allowed to be around you.

Now, this is one of the greatest revelations I have had in my life. Are you ready? If someone (and even a spirit) can only give you what is inside of them then this means that they are full of the same emotion they are feeding you. Which means that Hell itself, the demonic spirit of fear, is full of fear himself! But why? Demonic spirits were also there the day God expelled Lucifer from Heaven for becoming pride-filled and The Word of God tells us Lucifer fell from Heaven like lighting! There was no prolonged battle in Heaven when Lucifer began to believe he deserved God's position. And the Bible reveals that Lucifer then led a third of the angels to rebel with him against God. Demons are fallen angels. And these fallen angels who now are demons, have seen God. They know who holds the real power! They tremble at the power of Jesus! They are filled with fear and paralysis themselves! That's why when they come close they can only give to you who they are! That is exciting for those of us who follow Jesus! That is a testimony to His glory, power, and strength! Satan can only cause fear in you because he is full of fear himself and when he approaches you taste what fills his life -- Fear! Satan knows who is in charge! And it is not him!

You can taste it and experience it when demons come close much like you can lose your joy when you spend too much time around a joyless person. Now, conversely, when you speak to the spirit of fear in the Name of Jesus and command him to go, he has to go because demons must submit to the Name and Authority of Jesus. Then you are free to embrace intimacy with God's Spirit. And just like when you are around a person you taste of what's in them, you begin to taste what fills the Spirit of God and it rubs off on you! The Spirit of God empowers! The Spirit of God has no rivals or enemies that exceed Him in authority! So when you are led by the Spirit of God you experience a life free from the control of demonic fear. The fear that keeps you down. The fear that disables your faith to step. You can now begin to believe all things are possible to those who believe. You begin to understand you are next in line to do great things because God designed you to rule and reign on earth as His ambassador and representative.

That was the original plan in the beginning back in Genesis. We were never meant to be ruled by fear. We were to multiply and subdue the earth. We were to be God's representatives on earth, the extension of His power and rule. He yearned, and still yearns, for you to know who you are in Him! You are overcomers; you are winners; you are called and are to be triumphant! To succeed at what God has put in your heart. To be a connected part to an eternal Kingdom that will never fade, go away, or be conquered. You belong to the King of Kings and the Lord of Lords and if He is for you who can stand against you? WHO? King David says in the Psalms, "The Lord is my light and my salvation whom will I fear?" All of this hinges on who will you trust? Who will you trust to be in your life, to be around your life? Who will you allow to feed into you? Heaven? Or Hell?

Rick Warren has great insight into how trust affects faith. He says, "Faith is trusting God has a purpose for all that is happening in your life, without knowing why." Trust and fear are indicators. If you have fear there is no trust. This can become a cycle - fear, no trust, no trust, fear. But if you have trust you will not fear - cycle broken. You have to realize if you have fear in your life about ANYTHING, you are NOT currently in a trusting relationship with God who is the ONLY source of true peace.

> You can conquer the fear that holds you back & you can do great things. Because the God who designed you, designed you to rule over that fear.

Fear is the revealer that there is a lack of trust in your life when it comes to God. It is the sign that there is not only a lack of trust in God Himself but also in the gifts He has given you to accomplish the destiny He has planned for you.

Now, I am sure you have faith. It is just at times you have faith in the wrong things. You have trust; you just trust, at times, in the wrong things. Trust in God is the principle that prohibits fear. The word prohibit means: to forbid by law or authority; to hinder or prevent[34]. Luke 10:19 says this, "See, I have given you authority to tread on snakes and scorpions, and over all the power of the enemy. Nothing will harm you."[35] At times we all are a bit thick headed. Jesus had to say '*see*' to the disciples when they returned after driving out demons from people's lives. When you trust God above anything else and submit yourself to the Lordship of Jesus because you trust Him, you then have the authority of Heaven itself! To be a representative of the power of Heaven, just as the disciples were.

Fear is a bully. Nothing else. It pretends to have power over you, but it doesn't. You have to get militant with Hell! I believe God has brought you to this point so you will get fed up with being a punching bag for the lies of Hell. You do not have to take it anymore. Twisted Sister (a rock band from the 1970s-1980s) had a song called "We're Not Gonna Take It".

Although it was not a great song because it was fueling rebellion in general, I believe the root message of the song - that you have a right to choose what happens next - can be flipped for your good. At any point you can tell the spirit of fear *'I am not going to take it! I have a right to choose the direction of my life and I choose to go with God! I will align myself with who He says I am. I am not going to be bullied anymore, I have authority from the Creator Himself!'* You must grasp this truth. **Trust in God prohibits fear.** If you have a trust in God it is what allows you to live without fear. You have to build a trusting relationship with God to break the cycle of fear. There must be desire to stop going around being subjected to the same fears and anxieties every day. You have the power to put a stop to the cycle!

Practically, you must increase your time with Him in order to know Him, to be around Him and to hear Him. Wherever you are in making time for Him, increase it a little bit, maybe ten minutes a day. Your time reflects your priorities; it reflects where your trust is. If you are in a season where you are prayerless, the reality is you trust in your strength -- and it will fail you.

There is a way that seems right to man but in the end it is death. Relinquish control. Relinquish the future. Enjoy being a child of God and enjoy pursuing God. You will then find yourself on a crash course with your destiny because He will then move you into your purpose. The first step in becoming bold is being able to be intimate with God. To be able to know Him and trust Him in all things. To get rid of idols - things that you place in front of God. Tear down the idols. Get rid of anything that comes before God and your intimacy will be restored. And when intimacy and trust is restored, you will receive His Spirit in new measure and you will begin to see clearly and step boldly! Romans 10:11 says that those who trust in the Lord will never be put to shame. You will never go wrong trusting God! You will never go wrong stepping in faith and trusting God will make a way when there seems to be no way.

I want you to imagine with me right now a day without fear, a day in which you are filled with boldness, a life lived with confidence. Would that not be amazing? Would it not be awesome to live with confidence and boldness, without the presence of fear? This *IS* the way God designed it to be!! For in 2 Timothy 1:7 it says, "God has NOT given you a spirit of fear but of power, love and a sound mind..."[36]

God is a giver. Receive from Him. Be in proximity to Him. This is vital. It is so vital that if you cannot wrap your mind around the principle that *Trust Sustains Boldness* there is really no need in moving on to the next principle.

Everything hinges on trust in God. Faith hinges on trust in God. Boldness hinges on trust in God. Confidence hinges on trust in God. So, if you need to read this principle again in order to receive freedom in this area, then read it again and again while praying for a breakthrough in trust.

How will you know when your trust has been bolstered? You will see an increase of peace. You will see an increase of joy. You will receive an increase of love for God and for what He has in store. His Word tells you that no eye has seen and no ear has heard nor has it entered into the heart of man what He has prepared for those who love Him! That means as you trust Him you will begin to realize your thinking is too small.

Action Points to Strengthen My Faith to Power My Boldness:

1. _____

2. _____

3. _____

Pray this with me:

God, I need You. I need to trust You. Forgive me for relying too much on other things. I'm choosing to think differently starting today. I choose trust. I choose You. I want to be intimate with You starting right now, come close Lord Jesus and have Your way in me. Take my future. Take my life.

Thank You for leading and guiding me into my real identity and true purpose. Thank You Holy Spirit for filling me with new clarity and with enlarged dreams and visions. In Jesus Name. Amen.

Principle #8

Boldness Doesn't Bow to Barriers

The bold act when others won't.
Joel Brown

It is the bold who will act. The courageous that will step. Those who allow themselves to remain crippled by the spirit of fear do nothing great. Those who allow the cycle of negative '*what if's*' to rule their mind become stagnant in life. *What if* I step out and I fail? *What if* I take the risk and look foolish? *What if* I attempt what is in my heart and do not have what it takes to succeed? The merry-go-round of doubt in our minds is deadly. Sadly, most people are caught in this web of doubt. But they are not alone.

There are many, even those throughout the Bible who cowered in the moment they were called on to act boldly. Jesus chose Peter, a man with a history of embarrassing moments, as His first-round draft pick. Peter had left everything, literally everything he knew, to follow Jesus and the time had come for Jesus to go to the cross. Jesus had been arrested and it was Peter's moment to shine and admit wholeheartedly that he was one of the followers of Jesus! And to do it proudly. He was, after all, the star of the team, handpicked by Jesus Himself. I mean, he gave up everything for this moment, right? Jesus was now bound and being questioned, and Peter had followed closely behind to pry into the proceeding in order to see what was going to happen. During those moments, on three different occasions, he was pointed out as a follower of Jesus and each time he cowered. Each time he refused to stand up and be counted, and at one point even cursing at the top of his lungs because of the accusation and the accusers.

However, what is beautiful about the story of Peter is that he exemplifies how boldness works. Look at it this way, being in bondage or choosing freedom is like a fork in the road. You are always as close to going right as you are to going left. You are as close to winning as you are to losing. The lies of Satan make it seem that the only road to choose is left, the road of bondage, the truth is that when you are standing at the fork there is no difference in distance of either direction. You are one decision away from freedom. **At any given moment you can decide to be crippled by fear but at that same moment you can decide to go bold.**

This goes back to Principle One: You can choose at any point to live & think bold. Peter definitely broke out of his moments of doubt and led the church in Jerusalem with all courage, seeing thousands upon thousands come to Jesus, the very one he had denied. God is not a respecter of people; meaning He doesn't play favorites. He did not place the capacity to breakout of doubt and to step up in boldness in Peter alone. The same capability to change that was in Peter is in you -- the capability to look at obstacles and circumstances and dictate your own response. What I think is remarkable about Peter is that the obstacle he had to overcome was not the people pointing him out; the obstacle was within himself. He had to overcome his own thoughts and processes and thinking patterns that were prevailing in his life. Ultimately, he did not bow to those psychological barriers. I believe you, like Peter, are primed and ready for breakthrough. I believe you can step against all odds. I believe you were born for such a time as this.

So how do you live out your life in this generation? You must refuse to be driven by the spirit of fear and instead be driven by the Spirit of God. You must be: driven by faith, driven by purpose, driven by the desire to be effective in your day and in your time. You must not allow yourself to fall into being the person that allows life to dictate what you can and cannot do!

Do you realize Moses, the man who led Israel out of Egyptian slavery, is not here anymore? Where's the mighty

Biblical warrior Gideon? Where are the original disciples who did such great works and changed the course of history for the whole world? They're gone. Who is left? Who is alive right now that God wants to use in the same ways? You! Remember, God doesn't play favorites! He did not elevate and give power to some just so that the rest of us could look at them and go: '*Wow, they are special.*'

> Don't look at how big your obstacles are, see how big your God is and you will become an unstoppable force for the Kingdom.

NO! He did it because He is wanting to show you what He can do with you! You need to get it in your heart a and mind today that you have the same access to God Moses did, that Gideon did, that the great prophet Elijah did! Nothing is holding you back accept the choices you will make in regards to how you will live. Are you going to live by faith? Or are you going to live by sight? Meaning, you decide how you will step according to how you see the problem and how you see your ability. If you walk by how big the obstacles are you will never get out of the gate. But if you decide to see how big your God is, to know nothing is impossible to those who believe, to know that He will be with you as He was with the great men and women of the Old Testament, then you become an unstoppable force in a world that desperately needs you to engage. **The world needs your business, your book, your song, your ministry, your voice.** You are a unique creation of God, one-of-a-kind, priceless. Seek God by faith for the next step and take it. The bold do not bow to barriers.

In the Book of Daniel there is a story of a king and three young Hebrew men. The story goes that this king was so full of himself that he built a 90-foot gold statue of himself! And everybody was supposed to bow down to it when the music played. You have to realize this king was the king of Babylon at the time and Babylon ruled the known world. They were the superpower empire. You were supposed to take what they said and just roll with it. Can you image? I mean, think about it. If you were going to stand up against Babylon as a whole, you would have to carry a boldness like none other. And these three Hebrew boys did. The day came, the music started to play, and everyone started bowing down. You have to know that in their minds most people were thinking, 'This is stupid; how ignorant is it that our king is so prideful he thinks it's ok to build a 90-ft. gold statue of himself.' But the spirit of fear, the barrier of fear, kept them quiet and submissive to the moment.

But then there were the three. Three. Can you get this moment? It wasn't like the three had found a thousand people to boycott with them which might have given them a little leverage. There were no great multitudes they had convinced prior to this moment to go with them on their decision to defy the largest and greatest empire of the day. It was just them. Just three. And as the music played and everyone began bowing because of fear, it happened. The king saw his whole empire bowing and I can imagine the grin that came over his face. But hold on, what's going on over there? Those three men are refusing to bow? So, the king threw the three Hebrew boys into a furnace that was so hot the men ordered to throw them in died due to the heat. Yet, when the king looked into the furnace he saw something strange. He asked, 'Did we not throw in three? How is it I see a fourth? And he looks like the Son of God.' Yes! Jesus, God himself, met those three boys in that fire because they had faith and they had boldness. They refused

> God made you an overcomer of your failures, your past, and over your fear.
> Have faith in The God of Resurrection!

to bow to the barrier of fear. The boys were removed from the fire and scripture says they didn't even smell like smoke!

Listen, as you identify the spirit of fear and begin to defy it and step in boldness and faith; regardless of how you feel God will meet you. No one is going to be laughing at you in the end. They are going to be in awe of what God has done through you. Romans 10:11 says, "Anyone who trusts in him will never be disgraced."[37] God made you to be an overcomer! You might have failed in the past but that is over. Today is a new day. **The Spirit of God is in the resurrection business.** It is the Spirit of God that raised Jesus from the dead. The Spirit of God brings life where there seems to be none. That means if the *bold you* died or maybe even never existed to date, God can bring your boldness back to life or can birth new boldness in you.

You might say, '*But I have nothing for God to work with. I've never been bold. I have always been paralyzed to move.*' What you need to grasp is that God, your Maker, works best from nothing. In Genesis He said *let there be* and there was. That which He spoke was not in existence before He spoke it but it was after. It doesn't matter if you don't see where the boldness could even come from if you wanted it to, or where you would even conjure the courage to step in the area you need to step. The hinging point is faith. And faith steps even when it doesn't know the outcome. Try! Go for it! Even if you fail, like Peter, your failure isn't final. **You need to know that you are not identified by your failure; you are identified by your Father.**

Remember the Valley of Dry Bones? God, in the Old Testament, asked the prophet 'Can *these bones live?*' The prophet looked out over a valley full of dead men's bones and said, '*Only You know God.*' God told him to prophesy (to speak to) the bones and tell them to live. As the prophet did the bones began to rattle. Life came from absolute death. Flesh and tendons grew where there were none. The spirit of fear might have you in this moment believing your story is over, dead. That you have messed up too much, you have allowed a part of you to die that you believe can never be seen again. But I am here to tell you IT IS NOT OVER. Speak boldly over your future! As the prophet spoke boldly over the dry bones! Because that is what God has asked of you. He has asked you to

Rise up! For God will speak life into your visions, your dreams, and your future. Believe He can and He will!

understand He is a God of restoration. Believe today and He will begin even now to restore boldness in the same way He restored the flesh and strength to a dead army. In the same way He spoke energy and matter into existence to create a new world when it was not yet.

And God is telling me He wants to create a new world for you. A new way of seeing life. A way of seeing through the lenses of faith and boldness not fear and doubt. God is for you. He created you on purpose and with a purpose. And by the way, maybe you are reading this book and you have acted with a certain level of boldness to this point and you have actually done some great things by the grace of God. God is telling me to tell you think bigger. **Dream bigger. Go bolder.** This is a generation that will see an army rise up and take their place. To change culture, to change the world. The bold do not bow to barriers!

Action Points to Help Me Stand Strong:

1. _____

2. _____

3. _____

Pray this with me:

Father, I thank You that You create things from nothing. I thank You for boldness and faith. Spirit of fear you do not have the power anymore because God has given me authority over you in the Name of Jesus. Even though I may not see it yet I speak boldness into my life in Jesus Name. I choose to be identified by my Father and not by my failures. I commit to step into the unknown knowing God is with me and for me.

Principle #9

Bold People Break Barriers

There are no constraints on the human mind,
no walls around the human spirit, no barriers to our progress
except those we ourselves erect.
Ronald Reagan

It is imperative to understand that obstacles lead to opportunities if you have the right perspective -- the right attitude. Simply put, barriers are opportunities. For some, barriers are where they choose to stop. For others, where they choose to step. Breaking through barriers starts with your attitude; overcoming obstacles is a choice. It is up to you. For if there is one thing that rings true in life it is that you will either breakthrough or you will be broken by life. If you are broken by life you will sit defeated, breathing air but not living. You will be dreamless, hopeless, with no source of power to move forward. This is true for so many. And when I say so many, I mean most of those who are born into this world. So, each one of us has to do a gut check and ask: *Who am I? Who will I decide to be? Will life beat me into a place of defeat? Will defeat subdue me like an opponent in the ring that psychologically breaks my will?* Or... *Can I find the*

motivation, the will, the desire to overcome the things that would try to overcome me?

How's your gut check going? Are you intimidated by life? By the thought of stepping out? Has life beat you into submission? You must realize today that failure is temporary unless you quit altogether. Today you must realize that your obstacles, whether in business, in relationships, or in overcoming your past are merely opportunities before you to approach life in a different way, with a different mindset, and see the progress you have always desired.

> Realize today that failure is temporary unless you quit altogether.

One of my childhood heroes was a test pilot by the name of Chuck Yeager. If you have never heard of him before he is the test pilot that broke the sound barrier for the first time. He went supersonic, faster than the speed of sound. He did this by flying an experimental, untested aircraft called the *X-1*. It was a small rocket powered airplane that had to be attached to the underbelly of another larger aircraft, flown to the right altitude then dropped in order to commence its attempt at breaking past supersonic flight. Now, you might be reading this book saying, '*What is the big deal. He was just trying to go faster than sound; seems pretty straight*

forward.' However, the real story is that the pilots that had attempted this before Yeager had all 'bought the farm'; they all died. You see, as these pilots approached 760 miles per hour the plane would begin to shake and buffet wildly. The plane's integrity would be challenged, every bolt holding on for dear life because of the convulsing of the aircraft approaching this speed. It was called the sound barrier for a reason. And this barrier was invisible. You could not see it; it was not something you could visually identify. But the test pilots, along with NASA, knew of its existence because of the consistent deaths that were taking place because of it.

You see as the plane would approach the sound barrier the drag on the aircraft would increase dramatically. Simply put, drag is the force of resistance to moving forward. When drag increased the aircraft controls would become more unresponsive; it was harder to control the airplane. It was at this point, the point of greatest resistance prior to breaking through the invisible barrier, that the pilots would lose control and crash. However, on October 14, 1947, Chuck Yeager took on the sound barrier. As he approached it, the plane became increasingly unstable. Yeager, along with the *X-1,* was being pushed to the brink of losing control. Everything in him, and the plane, was being challenged by what some referred to as the *demon in the air.*

To make matters even more interesting, just before the day of his attempt, he had been thrown off of his horse while riding and had broken two ribs. This was a fact he kept to himself, only telling a close friend, because if it had come to light he would have lost his chance at being the one to face this challenge head on. He was in such pain and had such loss of mobility that his friend, who was also on this project, had to make him a special bar so that he could reach up and close the hatch to the plane. Without this self-constructed bar Yeager, due to his loss of mobility, would not have been able to close the hatch. With all this in mind you can understand the boldness it took to even attempt this feat. So many failures in trying up to this point; so many dead pilots. No promise of actually succeeding with an experimental untested aircraft and broken ribs. But even with all of these obstacles, one person saw opportunity and believed it could be done.

On that day Chuck Yeager pushed toward his invisible oppositions: a buffeting plane being thrown around in the air and excruciating pain coming from broken ribs. He did it! He faced his invisible enemy, pushed with everything he had in him, endured the pain and the fear of dying, and broke through. What is incredible is that the moment the sonic boom was heard, the sound that is made when a plane breaks the speed of sound, the aircraft immediately hit smooth air. In that moment, just a split second in time, it all went from almost losing all control to everything being as it should be – beautiful, serene, smooth sailing.

Fear acts much in the same way. It's invisible and it's a bully. It acts like it owns you as you approach certain areas of your life. But what if I told you it doesn't have what it takes to keep you from breaking through? **Fear is a bully that cannot keep you down if you will go bold.** If you will decide that through the pain, through the discomfort, through the doubts, through it all, nothing will stop you. Because you can be a pioneer just as Yeager was.

Decide that fear will not bully you and keep you down. You can be a pioneer and know that nothing can stop you!

The Apostle Paul was a pioneer. In order to tell the world about Jesus, he went through horrific moments. In 2 Corinthians 11 it tells us that he was beaten with rods three times, was put in prison and faced death constantly. He was robbed, and he literally was whipped multiple times without number, meaning he received so many strikes he couldn't even keep count. On top of that, he was stoned.

Acts 14 tells of the time when Paul and Barnabas were in Lystra doing miracles. This made the Jews from Antioch so mad that they came, stirred up the people in Lystra so much that they took him outside the city and stoned him. I think sometimes this part of Paul's life is overlooked; some of us just read Paul that was stoned and move on to what was written next. So, I have a question: have you ever had a rock the size of your hand thrown at you so forcefully that it actually made contact with your face? And not just once but over and over hitting you, stones hitting every part of you? And this goes on until the people hurling rocks at you think you are dead? Stop and think about what Paul endured and went through - the pain, the opposition. He endured just so that you (and I) could hear about Jesus! That Jesus loves you, is for you, and has equipped you to overcome any circumstance you might face as you pursue what He has put in your heart to do. What boldness and courage! What is even more incredible about this moment when Paul was stoned is that it says he got up and went back into the city! What? Are you kidding me? Was he nuts? Had he lost his mind? He just got stoned to the brink of death by people who hated his guts and he had the audacity to work himself back to his feet (after being left for dead) and walk back into the very city that had just thrown him out and stoned him! That my friend is boldness personified! Paul's tenacity, efforts, and life story made a way for innumerable people to push forward, to endure, to persist, to face their opposition and keep stepping.

And if there ever was someone who was bold, it was Jesus Himself. God Himself coming to earth to take on the wrath that was to be poured out on us because of our sin. To endure a Roman cross. To be ripped open and not say a word. And to buy for you and me the right to be empowered by His Spirit - not based on our merit but on His. Jesus Christ broke through. And He did so in order that you and I would have the same power and authority that He carried. Jesus Himself says in Luke 10:19 that He has given you all authority, that He has given you power to tread on scorpions and snakes, meaning demonic powers and yes, even the spirit of fear. He also goes on to say you have power to overcome all the power of the enemy!

So why then, are you afraid? Why are you paralyzed? Do you not know, have you not heard that the same Spirit that raised Jesus from the dead is in you and available to you if you trust and submit your life to Jesus? Breakthrough power! **The spirit of fear launches the greatest attack on what it itself fears the most. If you're being attacked relentlessly by the spirit of fear, know that the demonic spirit that is intimidating you is intimidated by you.** God has called you, ordained you, equipped you, and desires you to access the victory that is rightfully yours. You are a citizen of the Kingdom of Heaven. You have authority. You have the right to tell mountains to move in Jesus Name. And if you have not experienced your breakthrough yet, you can. Your breakthrough lies in you knowing your authority, the power that is working in you; it lies in knowing your rights as a citizen of the Kingdom. Jesus has given you authority.

But Jesus also said that according to your faith be it unto you. That means breaking through barriers rests on your faith. It's the bold who will breakthrough their barriers. **If you haven't seen yourself act boldly then the first step is to begin to think boldly!** Because you always live out the way you think. Are you tired of being a punching bag for fear? Punch back! Are you exhausted by doubt? Equip yourself with faith! You *can* overcome! You *do not* have to stay where you are. You *can* change. Who you were yesterday does not dictate who you are today. You can succeed. You can be the first at something, if you believe. If you are bold.

The beauty is that the breakthrough has already been purchased for you by Jesus. The key is agreement. The power

> Breaking through barriers rests on faith. To be bold, you MUST think bold!

for your life lies in agreement. What do I mean by that? The Bible says that you are saved when you 'confess' Jesus as Lord. The power for healing is when you 'confess' your sins one to another (declared in the Book of James). The word 'confession' is made from two Greek words: *homo* which means the same, and *logeo* which means word. So in essence, confession is saying the same words as God. Saying the same things as God. Simply put, it means coming into agreement; saying the things He is saying. As you do this, power is released. The problem is that you are bound by fear and defeat because you are agreeing with Satan. You believe his words: *I can't do it. I'll never break this addiction. I shouldn't write that book, who would listen to me? I am not qualified.* You see the problem? You are bound because you are not bold enough to believe God or say what He says about you.

Imagine if you began to say the same things about yourself and your circumstances as God says? It is, and will be a game changer for you! *I can do ALL things through Christ! Nothing is impossible to those who believe! I have authority to speak to mountains, meaning my obstacles and tell them to move out of my way!* As you change your thinking and you change your agreement from lies to the truth, you change. You begin to carry boldness. You begin to see the Spirit of God move through you to stand where others cower, to win where others lose, to accomplish where others give up. Commit to agreeing with God about who you are; go bold and see every barrier, seen and unseen moved out of your way. After all, bold people break barriers.

Action Points to Help Me Break Down Barriers:

1. _____

2. _____

3. _____

Pray this with me:

Father God, thank You for forgiving me for where I have agreed with the lies about who I am. Thank You for the ability to choose a new direction. Thank You for a new identity, for right now helping me realize that I can be bold and I can break through. I speak to you right now spirit of fear, your days of bullying me are over. Get out of my way in Jesus Name, I am coming through.

Principle #10

Boldness Awakens Greater Opposition

Hardship often prepares an ordinary person
for an extraordinary destiny.
C.S. Lewis

Misery loves company. Those who are not going anywhere do not want you moving ahead because it reminds them of their own lack of motivation. (Most of them are held back by fear; most are filled with fear.) This is what we saw in the story of Israel and the Promised Land. Out of the approximate two million original Israelites who came out of Egyptian slavery, only two entered into what God had promised. Of the twelve spies that were sent to spy on the land, only those two (Joshua and Caleb) had the courage to step in faith and believe God, go bold, and claim what was rightfully theirs.

The statistics are clear - most will never go bold and live by faith. But I believe that you do not have to be a statistic. At the end of the day **negative statistics are just the record of someone else's failure.** Someone else's bad decision in the moment. It is not a reflection or a prophecy about your future. You are free to make your own choices. But rest assured that those who choose a daily diet of failure with a side of discouragement will be sure to attempt to offer you a healthy dose of what they are feeding on.

Let me ask you a question. Have you ever noticed that when you get around someone that whatever atmosphere they are living in at that moment sloshes onto you? Think about it. Someone who is happy and joy filled walks into your office, shop, or home. They can't help but give you what they have. And they do, you begin to feel what is in them; you taste it and experience it within yourself. What was going on inside of them overflowed out of them and got on you. The same is true with someone who is depressed. After spending a few moments with them you walk out and go, "Wow! I need to go do something fun because that was heavy." People can only give you what they are full of. It is their native tongue. And when they speak negativity to you, it can get on you and into you if you are not careful.

On top of all that, the moment you decide to do something great, that is the moment you will be opposed, resisted, and mocked. There are spiritual enemies, a demonic realm that is in direct opposition to God's plan on earth and against you finding your purpose and living it out. The Bible gives many examples of this truth. As God was raising up David to be king, Goliath had to be dealt with at the same time. As Israel was stepping into the Promised Land, war and opposition was all they encountered. As Nehemiah gained a vision to rebuild the walls of Jerusalem, Sanballat and Tobias began to oppose him. As Daniel decided to humble himself, seek God, and gain understanding and wisdom, the Bible records that the Prince

> Who directs your steps? What voices do you listen to? Do not let opposition prevent you from fulfilling God's purpose in you.

of Persia - a demonic ruler - opposed the angel that was carrying God's answer for twenty-one days. But it is recorded in Daniel Chapter 10 that the angel told Daniel that from the day you purposed in your heart to humble yourself, your prayer was heard.

You can be sure of two things. One is that as you gain an understanding of how to break free from spiritual bondage, Satan will begin to oppose you with greater opposition whether it be in the spiritual world or through those he is controlling on this earth-other people. Two is that Heaven hears you and is moving into action because of your humility and understanding of how you actually win the fight. But with all that said, if you continue to pray and seek

God and if you will continue to step relentlessly, Satan stands no chance.

So, as well as having people oppose you, and on top of the opposition you face from spiritual demonic forces, you have a third enemy -- Yourself. The voices from yesterday come flooding in: *You have never done that before. You are not qualified; you don't stand a chance. Who are you to think you are something? Give up, it's going to fail; you will never lose the weight, pass the test, overcome the addiction!* The voice of your own intellect and reason begins blaring in your ears but does not have the power to hold you if you will move in spite of it. What would have happened if the Wright brothers had given into their opposition internally or externally? Airplanes would have had to have another inventor who could break through the noise of resistance, but

The world needs you to step out against the odds, dream your dream, know your God-given purpose, press on, & do it!

the outcome may have been delayed. What would have happened if Henry Ford had not stayed committed to his work? Someone else would have had to overcome the obstacles to making the first car. If Thomas Edison had given up on faulty design number 800 after all of his hard work and caved in to all of the voices around him that he was wasting his time, you and I would not have the light from a lightbulb to even read this book.

The World needs people who will, against all odds, push! People that will refuse to cave to fear, cave to the pressure to just be normal, and get a job just to have a job. The world needs people to step out. The world needs people who dream. The world needs YOU! Find your God-given purpose by spending time with Him, then DO IT! If it takes you twenty years do it! If it takes you fifty years, it's worth it. **No one can keep you from your purpose but you!** You have to make the choice who you will listen to, what voices will have the right to dictate your steps. Surround yourself with people who will champion you and not discourage you. This means you will have to say goodbye to some people in your life. Every relationship either adds, subtracts, multiplies or divides you.

Nehemiah refused to be distracted by his opposition. He made his team work with a weapon in one hand and their tool in the other. The problem is most of us think we are not going to encounter that serious of opposition and when it presents itself our jolted expectations drain us of all courage. You need to at every moment, no matter who you are around and how long you have known them, be ready to fight for what you see God has given you to do. Wait for it. Pursue with patience and boldness that which you know you are to do, and in time it will come. Defend your dream.

I love Habakkuk 2:2-3. It says, "The Lord answered me: Write down this vision; clearly inscribe it on tablets so one may easily read it. For the vision is yet for the appointed time; it testifies about the end and will not lie. Though it delays, wait for it, since it will certainly come and not be late." You need to get a picture of what you want to see in the future, a vision. Clarify it and write it down; wait for it patiently as you keep stepping towards it and rest assured it will take place.

Proverbs 16:3 says to commit your plans to the Lord and your plans will succeed. Now, what is interesting about this verse is this: the word plans in the original language is not just the word for plans, but it also carries the connotation of achievements. And this is where you need to pay attention. I am sure you have made plans and they have failed in the past. You did not feel the power of Heaven assisting you as you encountered opposition to what you were attempting to do. The problem might have been that you really wanted it for your own glory. You might have wanted to do something great so that you could find and have self-value. Glorify God and give Him the glory and praise in all things because you are already valued and great because of *whose* you are. You are great and valued because you are a special possession of God. And when you do not realize that, you begin to try to find greatness and value by elevating yourself (which is pride and an illegitimate way of living life and succeeding). So, God does not allow your plans to succeed.

But all is not lost. Starting today, humble yourself under the mighty hand of God and He will lift you up. Commit to give your achievements to God, the honor to God, and know you do not have to find greatness or value because you already have it. Then you will feel Heaven itself come empower your plans because you are secure in your identity. And it is in that security that He will give you the ability to overcome every obstacle. When your identity is right you know that you are an overcomer and no internal voice, external voice from a person, or voice from Hell can stop you because you are strengthened by the Holy Spirit of God. Everything you are aiming to do and accomplish will be attributed to God's power in you and not you yourself.

> You do not have to look for value, identity, or ability to overcome.
> You already have it! You have been strengthened by the Holy Spirit and with God's power in you, you can accomplish what you aim to do.

As you encounter these three levels of opposition you will become stronger and stronger. Resistance builds strength. Everyday millions of people subject themselves to hours at a gym, purposely engaging resistance. And what's funny is that a lot of people who are physically strong are not mentally strong; they have weak wills. I have had the privilege, since I live in the Hampton Roads area of Virginia (which is home to the largest military population in the United States) to talk to several men who have been in the Navy Seal community or who are attached to work alongside of them. And there is something I have heard repeatedly: these men are surprised at the ones who quit during training. The ones who showed up, who looked the part, appeared to be physical beasts, but did not have the fortitude to endure. You need to embrace resistance, not only physically for physical strength but also mentally for mental strength. Embrace the resistance. It will only make you stronger if you let it. Quit quitting!

There's a quote by an unknown author that says, "God doesn't give the hardest battles to his toughest soldiers; he creates the toughest soldiers through life's hardest battles." You can stand in a world that is busy bowing like the three Hebrew boys in the Old Testament who chose not to bow to the false idol when the music played. It says when the three boys did not bow, they threw them into the fire. You can say they met their opposition when they decided to stand for what they believed! But the king looked and said there is a fourth person in the fire. One with the appearance of the Son of Man! That was Jesus Himself! You too can stand and go bold. God will be with you as you stay submitted to Him. God will not abandon you when you are opposed if you will recognize Him as your source and as your God. He will make fools out of your enemies.

So again, how's your gut check going? Are you one who is going to shrink back because of unexpected opposition? Or are you one who will merely choose to work with your weapon in one hand and your tool in the other like Nehemiah? Expect opposition. But also, expect to overcome. Boldness awakens greater opposition. But only the bold breakthrough. You are different. You have the potential to rise. God has told you in His word to come out from among them (the world) and be different! You can be! You will be! There is no one who can oppose you as you step in faith and obedience that has enough power or authority to derail you. Do not conform to this world but be transformed by the renewing of your mind. You can!

Action Points to Make Me Strong in the Face of Opposition:

1. _____

2. _____

3. _____

Pray this with me:

Father, I recognize today that You have called me to live boldly. To face the opposition and to overcome. I commit to get rid of the naysayers and to surround myself with people who will speak life into me and to not be distracted by those who want to stay the same. I am great and valuable not because of what I do but because You are my Father. Everything I do from this point on will not be to seek greatness but to celebrate the fact that You are great and have included me in the story of victory. To You be all the glory for all of my future breakthroughs, in Jesus Name.

Principle #11

The Bold Fail,
But The Bold Do Not Faint!

It's hard to beat a person who never gives up.
Babe Ruth

Ever failed miserably? When you think back, can you feel the pain, disappointment, and shame? The deafening sound of this humiliation reverberates like an echo playing itself over and over within your heart and mind. An echo is a reflection of an original sound, and it arrives shortly after the original sound is made. In the context of failure - it is the thoughts and feelings that continue long after you failed. Echoes are usually weaker than the original sound but the echoes of failures that have not been dealt with seem to be the louder. The echoes of failure call out to you: *Don't try again! Don't trust again! Don't love again! You will only be hurt...again!* The echoes of your past have the power to paralyze your future, to stop you from boldly stepping out again and moving forward.

Seems a depressing way to open a chapter on a book that is supposed to encourage you to *Go Bold*. However, I am sure that at some point in your life, you have or are experiencing the echoes of failure. And you are not alone. Failure permeates the story of history - failure in relationships, failure in pursuing what's right, failure of leadership, failure of CEO's to lead with integrity, failure to love, failure to respect, failure to forgive, failure to be faithful. You name the failure and it has happened over and over as the centuries have passed. In your own life failure has been replete. You and I, if we were to sit and tell of all of our failures, we would exhaust hours upon hours because failure fills all the years we have lived. The emotions surrounding failure can be incredibly strong regardless of who you are; the time period you lived in; and your physical, financial, or spiritual circumstances. You can try to suppress the emotions, to forget about the situation. But many times you are unable to move on. Those experiences are when you are: FROZEN BY FAILURE.

So, what does being frozen by failure mean? Think about it. When you put something in the freezer, it immediately begins the process of trapping that item in its original state. It holds it there. The enemy's plan is for your failure to freeze you in that moment in time so that failure will remain in its original state. Satan wants you to run from your failure, hide your failure, even pretend it never happened. Because if you do not face it or deal with it, nothing changes. That part of your life will stay in a frozen state. **Failure freeze is the enemy's plan to reduce your future.** (If you want more information on escaping the bondage of failure, there is a great book in publication called *Failure Freedom: Understand Failure, Unlock Success* by Paul de Jong. Several of the things he talks about in his book concern moving beyond failure and into your destiny.)[38]

Failure is in everyone's world. As a matter of fact: the more committed you are to pressing forward, the more you will be exposed to failure. This is not to

> Satan wants to keep you frozen by your failures. God wants you to recognize that He made your DNA to overcome failure and step in your purpose.

discourage you but to remind you that *Failure is the only opportunity to begin again, only this time more wisely.*[39] Think about a baby that is about to take his/her first steps. You see them grab the coffee table in the middle of the room and you can see the determined look of their face as they begin to rise. Their legs are shaking; their arms are shaking, every part of them wobbling. But they will not be denied the chance to walk. You see it is in their DNA to overcome this moment. They take their first step and...you know and are expecting what happens next...yep, they fall. But even so, you don't stop cheering for them! Because you know they will walk as they keep trying. No one on this earth expects a baby to just start walking without falling. **Failure on some level should be anticipated, failure is what gives us the motor skills for success.** Thomas Edison said, "I have not failed. I've just found 10,000 ways that won't work... Many of life's failures are people who did not realize how close they were to success when they gave up." That is true about every part of your life as well. Advancement is the result of learning from failure.

Unfortunately, unlike the moment when you were a baby and your parents were cheering for you even as you failed, as you grow older the cheering slows down or stops altogether. Very few encourage you when you fall; no one cheers on the attempts you make. And sometimes you arrive at the place where you become crippled by your failure. But here are some questions to think about? Why did you stop getting up? Why did you stop trying? Why did you stop singing or writing? Why did you stop dreaming? Imagine for a moment if that baby I talked about decided to never get up

> Today, push harder through your failures. Pray through the hard stuff. Work to achieve your dreams. God is refining you for great things.

again. **You can't just give up because you have experienced failure....YOU MUST GET BACK UP!** Mark Twain said, "Most men die at 27, we just bury them at 72." You see, the world, failure, and the discouraging voices around us have a way of beating the dreams out of us at a very early age. We then resort to living lives that are monotonous, risk free, and ultimately reward free. Life is reduced to mere existence, ruled by failure and by fear.

Is this you? Is this where you are in life? Dreamless? Visionless? Faithless? Then allow God to take you on the journey of processing your failure! Do not ask God, '*Why?*' Ask Him, *'What for?'* Because there is something He is going to teach you, something He is going to refine in you, some skill that will be honed so that the next time you try you will go further and farther than ever before. This is easier said than done. But to achieve great things, you can and will have to push harder than you thought you would have to push! The day you want to close down your business, the day you want to throw away your marriage, the day you want to quit school, the day you want to stop working on writing your book - whatever the circumstance - you will have to *Go Bold* and push through! You will have to pray through!

Jesus talked about praying through. He said ask and it will be given, knock and the door will be opened, seek and you will find. As you read these words you may have the tendency to believe that the span of time for asking the Lord about something is relatively short. However, the Greek translation for what He said tells a different story. The original language of the New Testament tells you to keep asking, keep seeking, keep knocking! This tells you that you are to be relentless.

Relentlessness is an attribute of the successful. It separates the men from the boys (and the women from the girls). It divides the ones who will make it from the ones who will not. If you cannot develop the attribute of relentlessness, you are going to lose at life. Relentlessness says "I don't care what happened today; I'm getting up tomorrow and doing it

> You were created to be relentless: to push past the barriers, push past the fear, push past the rejection. You were created to be relentless!

again!" It is the ability to suffer greatly, be immensely stretched, be down and out, and still with all your strength make another push! To push into the future regardless of fear. To push into new relationships regardless of past rejection. To push past doubt and see all you know you are to do accomplished. **Relentlessness gives you sight; it sees through discouragement, fear, and failure.**

The Israelites wandered in the desert for 40 years after God led them out of Egypt and most of them were internally defeated. They could not muster the strength to even think about entering what God had promised, the land of Canaan. They saw themselves as grasshoppers in their own eyes. They were stuck in a place of defeat. But, with them were Joshua and Caleb! Caleb translated means *wholehearted*! And with his whole heart He believed God over the current circumstance. With his whole heart He saw the future beyond his present; he did not use the past failures to paint the picture of what was about to happen next. The Bible says Caleb had a different spirit. It was that relentless spirit to believe against all doubt that he was going to make it into his purpose and destiny regardless of what anyone else chose to do. And he did! Out of the approximate two million original Israelites that came out of Egypt that were supposed to step by faith into the Promised Land of Canaan, only Joshua and Caleb were allowed to lay hold of that promise (along with the successive generation).

Narrow is the way to life and few find it, Jesus said. And to the seven churches in Revelation He said it is the overcomer that will receive the promises of God. The one who will overcome, the one who will hold on to his faith when no one else does is the one who will get up and do it again with

129

everything in them and trust God that breakthrough is on its way! The one who chooses a different spirit than the world - a courageous spirit, a spirit that doesn't quit, a spirit of relentlessness - That is the spirit I am calling out of you right now in Jesus Name!

You are created to be relentless, to be like your Heavenly Father who painted a picture of relentlessness when He wrote the story of history. He has been and is patient with humanity. He is always willing to go through the highs and lows with each us and still pursue us. He is willing to give you new mercies everyday so that you might come to Him, so that in the end His purpose will be fulfilled.

> Don't fear. Don't worry. Don't quit!
> God designed you;
> God purposed you;
> God will pursue you!
> You are loved!

The Spirit of God is eternal; He doesn't "quit". The Spirit of God is not intimidated by anything and you as one of His sons or daughters, you have that as an inheritance - because the apple doesn't fall far from the tree! The problem is you forgot whose tree you came from – that you are fearfully and wonderfully made, exquisitely designed, powerful, purposed for greatness, and loved by God!

So don't ever quit. **You are closer today than ever, so hold on.** To win at life, to do great things, you will need boldness. The bold fail but the bold do not faint. If you feel tired, don't worry; it won't kill you. If you feel like you are in a season of fear, don't fear; for seasons come and go. If you feel defeated, realize that is only an attitude that can be changed and that you do have a choice.

Today can be different. Choose this day to be different, to fight, to resist your opposition and re-engage. The battle, the victory, and the promise go to the wholehearted. Go after what God has given you, inspired you to do, set in your heart. And do not let any voice deter you. You were made to be great! Nothing is impossible to the one who will believe.

Action Points to Help Me Stand:

1. _____
2. _____
3. _____

Pray this with me:

Thank You, Jesus, for giving me the power and revelation to understand that I can step out again. Breathe into my dreams once again. Thank You that today I realize that I have the ability and choice to get up out of my discouragement. That I have the opportunity to try again

after learning from the past and from areas where I have failed. Thank you Jesus for making me relentless. I refuse to allow my past to dictate my future. I choose to go bold.

Principle #12

Boldness is Not About Knowing Every Step, But About Knowing The One Who Orders Your Steps

*...the more you make the choice to live above your feelings, to
trust God instead of what you may feel like doing,
the stronger your faith becomes. It's not about being perfect.
We will always be on a journey of growing closer to God.*
Tim Tebow

There is something that shifts inside of you when you understand how great and powerful God is. There's something that changes inside of you when you grasp that the one and only Creator God, who is all-powerful, is for you.

I can remember back to when I was eight years old. My family and I were living in Lima, Peru, because my parents were serving there as missionaries. I was outside on the playground that was right outside our apartment building. Now, I was a loud-mouthed kid back then; I had a problem with acting tougher and bigger than I really was. On this one particular day I picked a fight with a couple of boys that were a bit older than me and a whole lot bigger than me. As the situation got more heated I just kept egging it on and I quickly realized that the situation was not going to turn out well for me. Especially because, even as tough as I thought I was, the fact of the matter was that it wasn't just one kid but multiple kids I had roused up. And I was going to have to face them on my own. The moment was rapidly approaching where fists were inevitably going to fly, and it was at this moment that fear took a hold of me. I could not see myself getting through this moment well, and this fear was being fueled by the fact that I was not powerful enough to win the fight I was about to enter. I wanted to turn, tuck my tail, and run! Just then, as all this was happening, my older brother (who was larger than me *and* the boys I had antagonized) came up behind me; he stepped in front of me and in just a few seconds the confrontation was over. Those boys did not want to pursue the fight any longer because someone bigger and stronger had just shown up on the scene. Even though just seconds before I was terrified at the thoughts of what these boys were about to do to me for being a punk kid, when my brother stepped in and I knew the pressure was no longer on me. Man! I tell you, a boldness rose up in me (as I stood behind my brother) and I shouted some final words: "Yea, that's right! Run off!" I mouthed off one final time as if I had anything to do with their newfound fear.

This story exemplifies how godly boldness works. It's not based on your power, but His. Proverbs 28:1[40] says, "The wicked run away when no one is chasing them, but the righteous are as bold as a lion." Why the righteous? What does righteousness even have to do with being bold? The word *righteous* plainly means being in right standing with God. If I had not had a good relationship with my brother, if there wasn't a true connection or love between us, he would have never stepped in for me. On the contrary, he would have stood back and watched his punk kid brother get lined out, humbled and hurt. So it is with the all-mighty, all-powerful Creator God. When you are in right relationship with Him, He intervenes and steps out in front of you and paves the way for you to overcome. Even when you have put yourself into a predicament. You should not make this a habit but even when you do find yourself in a place of fear that you created, if God knows your heart is truly on Him and that you desire Him and love Him, He has no problem being your Deliverer. That is part of His nature.

Many of you reading this book right now are experiencing paralyzing fear. You might have picked up this book as a last attempt to break out of the grip of the spirit of fear. And guess what - if you want freedom it's available! I believe that right now God is solidifying the picture He wants you to have of Him. You see, **God is your Helper. Sustainer. Defender. Leader. Guide. Deliverer. Rescuer. Redeemer. Provider. Father. Friend. Fortress. Security. Peace. Designer & Owner of all the earth and He has sworn to fight the battles of those who trust Him.**

Jeremiah 20:11 says, "But the LORD is with me like a violent warrior. Therefore, my persecutors will stumble and not prevail. Since they have not succeeded, they will be utterly shamed, an everlasting humiliation that will never be forgotten."[41] Can you get that in your spirit? God is a violent warrior! And He is violent against the opposition that comes against His children. God Himself has no opposition. Scripture tells us that as many as believed in Him, Jesus,

> Put your heart on God, your Deliverer, your Helper, Leader, and Guide. Let Him be the one who fights your battles, paves the way, and breaks your fears.

God gave the right to be His children! No one can stand before God or come against His will. So, if God is for you who do you think you need to fear? What situation do you think is insurmountable? Why are you depressed? Why are you discouraged? It is time to raise your head! Time to depend on God like never before and to celebrate who He is. It is time for you to regain your awe of His power and strength.

You see, when the Bible says the wicked run away when no one is pursuing them it means that there are things that can rule over your life when you are separated from God. Fear is allowed to rule over you. Anxiety is allowed to rule over you. Discouragement is allowed to rule over you. And even though you might have prayed the prayer of salvation that does not mean you have a free pass in this life to the power God has promised. **You might be saved by your confession about who Jesus is, but you can be saved and still be bound up.** The Bible says in Thessalonians, do not quench the Holy Spirit. The Greek word for quench seen here means *to extinguish or suppress.* One of the main things I look for in my life to make sure I am connected to the Holy Spirit and have a good relationship with Him is His fruit. Galatians chapter five talks about the fruit of the Holy Spirit of God. The first three are key: love, joy, and peace. There are more but these are my personal three indicators. If there is no love in my life, no joy, and no peace, even though I might have surrendered my life to Jesus I can say on some level our relationship is a bit estranged. My eternity might be secure, but my soul is in bondage.

Why can someone be saved and still in bondage to fear? Because somewhere down the line the enemy has lied to them and they have held onto that lie over God's truth. I tell

Christians who continually battle with depression, fear, and worry that there is only one problem - they don't truly believe God. That is a tough pill to swallow especially if they are someone who may have Bible verses plastered all over the bathrooms, kitchens, rear-view mirrors, and even have them memorized. Anyone can quote all the right scriptures but when I look into their eyes I see rejection, insecurity, and doubt. What's the problem? They have the information about who God is, but they do not believe it deep down. They think they believe because their mind knows The Word, but it is not knowledge of God's Word that frees us.

You might be getting sideways with me right now because in your mind you are saying, "But Joel, the Bible says that *'...you will know the truth and the truth will set you free.'* So it *is* knowledge of God's word that frees us." Sadly, that is not the truth. The power of God is released when you do not add to or subtract from His word and you pay attention to all that He has said. That verse actually reads, "IF YOU HOLD to my teaching, then you really are my disciples (followers). THEN you will know the truth and the truth will set you free."[42] If someone is being held captive by fear, they are "holding" to lies and not "holding" onto the truth. This is why people can give their life to Jesus, be saved eternally, and still be in bondage. Because as soon as Satan lies to them about who they are, what he says the future holds, and what they can or cannot do and they listen to Satan instead of "holding" to who God is and what He has said, they "hold" onto those lies as if that was the truth. They believe Satan over God. Many well-meaning Christ followers are being bound by fear and it's simply because ultimately they do not believe God over Satan.

So today, if you come to grips with the fact that you have just not believed God, you are about to break into freedom. Ask God's forgiveness for believing Satan over Him. Ask His forgiveness for quenching the Holy Spirit, putting out His power in your life due to doubt. And commit to never believe Satan over God again. Make a commitment to "hold" to who God is, The One who goes before you and paves the way for your victory. The One who will never leave you or turn His back on you. The One who made you with a sure future is ready to lead you to it, and He delights in fighting for you if you will stop trying to control life and trust Him. Even now, as you are re-engaging your faith, strength is coming back to you. Even now I command new vision and

> God is The One who goes before you and paves the way for your future. God is The One who will always be with you, fighting for you. Rest on His strength.

dreams to come to the forefront. I speak to the dead dream you have let go of because you doubted it could come to pass and I speak life into it once again! **You can...even if you haven't because the outcome does not rest on your strength but on God's.** Much like the outcome on the playground that day did not come from me but came from someone bigger and more powerful than me!

Life is not that complicated. Life is not meant to be depressing. Scripture says in 1 John that you are called to prosper! But you may say, "I don't see the light at the end of the tunnel." "I can't see how I am going to win this battle." "I don't see how the promises I feel God has spoken to me are going to be realized." I want to speak to this for a brief moment as this book winds down.

What if I told you, you do not have to chase your dreams? Let me share a truth with you right now. Purpose precedes production. God is not in Heaven wondering what He might be able to do with you. He already designed you with intent and purpose before you were born. Just like anything that is manufactured it is intentionally designed on the front end for a specific end purpose, a specific use. And if it comes from a quality designer the product has immense value. But what if the designer is God, perfect in all His ways and wise beyond comprehension? How perfectly are you put together to accomplish the things He has placed in your heart? No one can stand in your way unless it's you! This happens the moment you choose to quit or doubt God.

Let me ask you a question. If you are going to receive an inheritance, do you have to chase after it? Do you have to do something for it? No, you just wait patiently because at some point it comes to you. Your success, as you trust God and let Him lead you, is a promise. The dreams and visions He has

> God, the Creator, isn't wondering what He can do with you - He designed you with intent and purpose before you were born. You have immense value, perfectly put together to accomplish the things He has placed in your heart.

put in your heart about your future are promises of where He wants to take you. And God's promises are based on Him fulfilling them. They are actually an inheritance for being His son or daughter. Hebrews chapter six says to be imitators of those who inherit promises through faith and perseverance. Did you catch that? **Promises are not meant to be chased after but inherited.** Hebrews goes on to say that God promised to bless Abraham and multiply him, and after waiting patiently, Abraham obtained the promise. You can't make your God-given dreams come true, and God never meant you to work that hard for them. He is a good Father who wants to bless you and lift you up as you stay humble under His hand. He wants to fight for you like a violent warrior; He wants to go to bat for you and win you the battle without you having to lift a finger. Sound too good to be true? It is true. Your job is to love God and love people. As you do this you fulfill what He asks of you. Then, because of honoring Him, you as His child receive His favor. The Old Testament declares what God has said, "...those who honor Me, I will honor, but those who despise me will be disdained." So... Stop worrying. Stay confident. Wait patiently. Keep your faith full by "holding" to the promise God has given you about your future -- that it will be good and that you will be significant. Glorify God at all times and see Him orchestrate your inheritance. He will bring about the reason you were born and you will impact the world with such a force that no one will be able to deny your value. **Boldness is not about knowing every step, but about knowing The One who orders your steps.**

Action Points to Help Me Know & Follow God's Path for Me:

1. _____

2. _____

3. _____

Pray this with me:

Lord Jesus I trust You. I thank You that I do not have to worry. I thank You that You are good. I thank You that You are intimately involved in my life. I will not follow how I feel, what I think, or my own wisdom. I chose to recognize that You are present in every moment and that You will speak to me, lead me and guide me. Thank You that because You are showing me who You are and who I am I can trust You at all times. And that trust thrusts me into living boldly. I thank You that I am next in line to do great things. Holy Spirit let's go impact the world!

The Lagniappe (13th) Principle

Relentlessness Separates the Ones Who Make It From the Ones Who Will Not

You can...even if you haven't.
Joel Brown

One thing you need to know about me is that I am a Cajun. I was born in New Orleans, Louisiana. We have a term in the South: Lagniappe (pronounced lan-'yap). It is a word that is used to signify one extra, a baker's dozen, instead of twelve. It's *the let's do thirteen for good measure* principle. It is also defined as something given as a bonus or extra gift. So, I am going to cover a thirteenth principle for good measure as a gift to you. That principle is this: **Relentlessness separates the ones who make it from the ones who will not**. Plain and simple: People who give up lose out. People who will not persevere crumble and fade into the distance as those who will cease to have an impact on the world for the better.

Most every success story is a story of someone who, against all odds, stepped out another day and pushed against opposition. Even when they are at the point they feel like they do not have what it takes, they get up and do it again.

They go years with this mindset until one day their dream is realized. For your success story to be realized, you will not just encounter a little opposition you will encounter years, possibly decades, of opposition. And after you have seen success in some areas you will set your sights on bigger goals; and yes, you will experience more opposition. Get used to it! It's part of being in a spiritual battle that's being played out with earth as its stage. But if you can hold on against doubt, if you will get up and try again, if you will not allow your critics to silence you, the world will make way for you simply because you are clear and committed to seeing what is inside you come out. Simply because you are not going to give up, roll over and play dead. Galatians 6:9 states this principle. It says, "So we must not get tired of doing good, for we will reap at the proper time if we don't give up."[43]

It's easy to come to the place where you lose it, throw your hands in the air, and ask *why bother*. I have, in the past, found myself even asking, "What's the point"? In Revelation Chapter 2, Jesus is speaking to seven specific churches and this is what He says repeatedly to them: the victor (meaning the overcomer, the one who perseveres to the end), that person will receive what I have promised. Are you catching the message? There are no good promises to the one who does not overcome. You need to get back up! You must try again! You can't allow defeat to conquer you. Why? Because the promises of a good and all-powerful God await you! If you don't fight the good fight and overcome, the prize does not go to you; it will slip right out of your hand.

Overcoming is also directly connected to salvation. Now, in Philippians 2:12 Paul tells us to work out our salvation with fear and trembling, meaning, that there are levels of salvation that require process. Did you know that? Let me explain. The Greek word for salvation in this passage is the word *sótéria*, and it has multiple connotations not just one. It is used to administer the idea of deliverance as well as salvation. When most Christians think of salvation they might think immediately of eternal security, but by doing so they limit the work God wants to do when it comes to their salvation AND DELIVERANCE. You see God wants you delivered and free in the here and now as well as eternally secure with Him. He has not called you to stay in bondage. Salvation is not limited to a mere futuristic moment where you do not go to Hell, but it has relevance to your daily life today because the word salvation denotes freedom! Freedom:

> The promises of a good and powerful God await you!
> Don't give up.
> Don't quit.
> The prize awaits you.

Deliverance from fear, doubt, insecurity, depression and a visionless life. So, do you want to accept eternal security but not overcome your current enemies? Probably not. You see, there are levels and you must stay engaged in the process to experience ultimate freedom and victory. That is why Paul says *work out your sótéria*, get free from bondage as you await an eternity with God. Be in relentless pursuit of all God has for you; do not fall short of what you could have today.

The dreams and visions God has placed in your heart are yours to experience; they are meant to become reality. God did not design you for a specific role and purpose in life and then change His mind. Romans 11:29

> God is not one who changes His mind and takes back His gifts. Your dreams and visions, the ones He placed in your heart, are the ones He wants you to fulfill.

says that God's gifts and callings are without repentance. Repentance just meaning a change in mind or thinking differently. So plainly it means, God will never take away from you the gifts and callings He has placed on you or given to you. He will never change His mind about who you are or what you were meant to accomplish because He settled that the day He made you. So, no matter how far you have fallen into hopelessness or how exhausted you feel you can find freedom, deliverance, and the power to re-engage.

In moments of weakness rely on God who can and will do in you what you are not capable of doing yourself. Do not dwell on your limitations or moments from the past when you have felt defeated or lost. Capture the negative thoughts and change them! Where you win or lose FIRST occurs at the location of the biggest battle - BETWEEN YOUR EARS!! Your thoughts will either limit you or liberate you. The Lord says in Isaiah 43:18-19, "Do not cling to events of the past or dwell (think) on what happened long ago. Watch for the new thing I am going to do. It is happening already — you can see it now!"[44]

How do you do this when you are overcome with thoughts of fear, failure, and defeat? You fix your thoughts. On what? Philippians 4:8 gives you one main key to help do this, to help you find the strength to try again. "Fix your thoughts on what is true, and honorable, and right, and pure, and lovely, and admirable. Think about things that are excellent and worthy of praise."[45] The main key is thinking on what is true. What drains your passion for life and purpose? Lies. Satan will fill your mind with lies like: *It is just too much for me, I can't. There's no way I can go on. I don't have what it takes.* All of these are lies. Truth is: God is for you. God delights in you. He is not finished with you. He will lead you through everything no matter what it might be. Remember this, what energizes you with passion and purpose is the truth. You can overcome. You can get up. God made you to fight. He made you an overcomer. The question is, will you recognize today that you are one?

Maybe right now you can't see yourself as an overcomer. Maybe you are at the point that you want to give up or realize that in the past you have not had what it takes to stay focused and relentless. Maybe you are close to calling it quits. Don't! Because I believe you are a different kind of breed. I believe you are relentless. Even if you do not see it in yourself the potential is there, and I know it even if you don't.

The choice is yours. You can stay where you are, or you can break out. Relentlessness is a choice, nothing else. Relentlessness

> God is for you.
> He loves you.
> He delights in you.
> You are an overcomer!

is more than knowledge; it is a heart issue. Relentlessness is the drive to get up every day and do it again. And in order to do that there must be passion and Godly stubbornness. For nothing great ever happened within your comfort zone. For in order to step out boldly, and in order to continue to live fiercely for God and for the vision in your heart, you must be *relentless* in your effort. Webster defines relentless as: 'showing or promising no abatement [decline or reduction] of severity, intensity, strength, or pace'.[46] In other words, you must be persistent, not easily bent or swayed. Hebrews 10:39 says that we who are relentless, "are not those who draw back and are destroyed, but those who have faith and obtain life." You need to understand that relentlessness is a value God insists on seeing within you.

> Be fierce in pursuing your dreams. Live boldly for God. He expects to see you being relentless.

There are eight (8) things that God has said to you that if you take to heart will launch you into a bold and relentless mindset:

1. I love you with an everlasting love (Jeremiah 31:3)
2. I am the God who forgives all your sins (Psalm 103)
3. I have called you by your name (Isaiah 43:1)
4. Come to Me when you are tired and burdened and I will give you rest (Matthew 11:28)
5. You are a mountain mover (Mark 11:22-3)

6. Do Not Fear (Isaiah 41:10)

7. I have made you complete (not lacking anything) (Colossians 2:10)

8. I make all things new (2 Corinthians 5:17)

Remember though, you will not just wake up tomorrow morning and suddenly be free forever from the spirit of fear. As the truth gets deeper and deeper in your heart and your belief becomes galvanized within you, you will experience greater levels of salvation in the here and now, meaning you are delivered daily on a greater level. You have to have patience; things do not just happen immediately sometimes. And you have to have persistence. James 1:12 says, "A man who endures trials is blessed, because when he passes the test he will receive the crown of life that God has promised to those who love Him." So stay on course. Persevere. Stand for faith and hope even against what you see with your eyes. Also know that relentlessness takes perspiration - you have to sweat. Nothing is gained with the attitude of entitlement. "Lazy people want much but get little, but those who work hard will prosper."[47] Some of the victory over fear lies on you. There is no great ending without hard work. But it is all so worth it! **You can, even if you haven't yet!**

About the Author

Ordained to ministry September of 1999 Joel Brown was on staff at Keypoint Church in Northwest Arkansas as the worship pastor over two campuses. It was September of 2011 when God began to stir Joel's heart to plant a church in Chesapeake, Virginia - a city over 1200 miles away from where he and his family had called home for so long. Joel packed up a 24 foot trailer and his family and founded Church at Hampton Roads September 16th of 2012.

Born 1975 on Napoleon Avenue in New Orleans, Louisiana, Joel has known ministry his entire life; his parents were staff pastors at an influential church in New Orleans then later with Joel and his brother, served as missionaries in the countries of Peru and Haiti before relocating to Northwest Arkansas in 1990. It was there that Joel met his wife, Sarah who currently serves as Co-pastor of Church at Hampton Roads.

Married January 1996, they have three children who also serve within the church: Hannah, who serves as Worship Team Coordinator; Bethany, who leads worship and coordinates the high school ministry; and Josiah, who is the lead drummer on the CHR Worship Team.

Joel Brown is driven by one word: others. It is the basis of the mission of CHR: Leading people into connection and full devotion to God. This is the heart of Joel Brown: "My only goal is to live my life boldly for the glory of my Lord and Savior Jesus Christ. To know Him and to be known by Him."

Endnotes

1 Capitalization added
2 A Conversation With Robert Frost (1952). NBC New.s Resource Type: Video Documentary [Long Form Specials/Datelines, etc.]. Creator: Bela Kornizer. Copyright: NBCUniversal Media, LLC. Event Date: 11/23/1952. Copyright Date: 1952
3 www.google.com. Google dictionary online
4 https://www.merriam-webster.com/dictionary/bravery
5 John 18:10
6 Mark 8:33
7 Luke 22:54-62
8 Acts 2:14-32
9 Acts chapters 6 and 7
10 Matthew 9:29 (KJV)
11 Mark 9:23
12 Luke 24:49
13 NLT
14 www.brainyquote.com/quotes/quotes/b/benjamindi122124.html
15 www.thomasedison.com/quotes.html
16 Isaiah 6:8
17 Isaiah 26:3 NLT
18 NKJV
19 Revelation 12:10-11 NLT
20 Revelation 12:12 NLT
21 New Living Translation (NLT)
22 Songwriters: Claude Francois, Gilles Thibaut, Jacques Revaux, Marcelo Drumond Nova
23 See Judges Chapter 7
24 Aesop
25 Author Unknown
26 NLT
27 NLT
28 HCSB
29 Proverbs 13:20
30 Brackets added.
31 Romans 10:17
32 NKJV
33 Joshua 3:5
34 https://www.merriam-webster.com/dictionary/prohibit
35 BSB

[36] Capitalization added

[37] NLT

[38] Publisher: Paul de Jong Ministries. 2015.

[39] Henry Ford

[40] NLT

[41] CSB

[42] John 8:31-32 (NIV). Capitalization added.

[43] HCSB

[44] Good News Translation; parentheses added

[45] NLT

[46] www.merriam-webster.com/dictionary/relentless

[47] Proverbs 13.4. NLT

Made in the USA
Middletown, DE
06 December 2018